Valentine's Day History

How to Celebrate Valentine the Right Way

(Brief History of Valentine Including Interesting Facts About Valentine's Day)

Alfonso Barton

Published By **Kate Sanders**

Alfonso Barton

Valentine's Day History: How to Celebrate Valentine the Right Way (Brief History of Valentine Including Interesting Facts About Valentine's Day)

ISBN   978-1-9992555-3-4

No part of this guidebook shall be reproduced in any form without permission in writing from the publisher except in the case of brief quotations embodied in critical articles or reviews.

Legal & Disclaimer

Table Of Contents

Chapter 1: Biblical Origins Of Valentine's Day

Valentine's Day is a day of celebration that honors romantic love among two people. The tour's roots can be observed within the Bible, no matter the fact that it is able to have taken on more secular traits throughout time.

The Book of Esther inside the Bible includes the Valentine's Day narrative. In this narrative, the King of Persia chooses the younger Jewish maiden Esther to be his partner. The excursion is found because of Esther's bravery and braveness in status up for her humans.

In the Bible, feasting and rejoicing have been to be found on the fourteenth day of the Jewish month of Adar. This is idea to be how Valentine's Day was given its start. The birthday party of in the intervening time has advanced over time, and now consists of giving and receiving gambling cards, plants, and offers.

The price of showing love and problem for each other is also pressured within the route of the Bible. "Love is affected person and mild," in keeping with 1 Corinthians Valentine's Day is a time at the same time as couples show their love and admiration for each one of a kind with the aid of changing tokens of their affection.

Additionally, the Bible discusses the price of marriage and the manner human beings could likely end up one in God's eyes. This is also venerated on Valentine's Day at the same time as couples make public commitments to every other or renew their vows to every other.

Valentine's Day may have advanced over the years to have a more secular this means that, however the Bible is wherein all of it started out. The Bible emphasizes the importance of affection and care, which may be every celebrated in this particular day every yr.

The Bible emphasizes the fee of self-sacrificing love, and Valentine's Day is historically placed as a day to have a tremendous time this form of affection. The Bible instructions us to "love our neighbor as ourselves," and Valentine's Day is frequently seemed as a day to express our love and gratitude to folks that are close to us. In addition, the Bible says that "love covers a mess of sins," and that is additionally commemorated on Valentine's Day at the identical time as couples display their gratitude for and forgiveness of each other.

Valentine's Day is a day to honor God's love as nicely. This is a day to apprehend and replicate on God's unwavering love for every person, this is a few element the Bible mentions. This day offers us a chance to explicit our love for God and to offer thanks for His love.

Valentine's Day's origins are determined inside the Bible, no matter the reality that it has superior proper right into a extra secular holiday inside the course of time. We can see how the Bible has precipitated this unique

3

day's celebration, from Esther's bravery to like's sacrifice. Couples all internationally are reminded of the price of love and being worried for every other on Valentine's Day, as well as of the need to be satisfied about God's unwavering love.

Valentine's Day is a time to honor the charge of friendship. A buddy loves commonly, in line with a verse within the Bible. We can also additionally express our gratitude for their love and help on this important day by manner of showing our appreciation for our pals and family. This day gives us the opportunity to each deepen and forge new ties.

Valentine's Day is an occasion to keep in mind the price of self-love. Love your neighbor as your self, steady with the Bible. We have to use this current to exercise self-care and to explicit our love and recognize for ourselves. This is an possibility for us to pay attention on our aspirations and to make smooth resolutions for the destiny.

Valentine's Day is a time to honor all sorts of love, collectively with the love of pals and the affection of God. It is an afternoon to reflect on the charge of self-love, sacrificial love, and disturbing for others spherical us. Today is a time to have a top notch time Esther's bravery and bravado in cutting-edge, further to to present way to God for his unwavering love. On this extraordinary day, we is probably reminded of the wonder of love and the techniques in which it may enhance our lives and offer us consolation.

The Story of Esther

Esther modified right into a more youthful little one who resided in a small village. She had in no way placed Valentine's Day, however she had commonly fantasized of doing so.

Esther got here upon a sign advertising and advertising a Valentine's Day party in the destiny while she modified into taking walks via the network. She couldn't wait to move away considering that she become so excited.

She changed into astonished to obtain at the birthday celebration and word all the decorations and attendees dressed to the nines.

Esther had a cute night time. Together together together with her friends, including some new ones, she danced and laughed. Everyone end up especially warm temperature and friendly. She obtained a solitary purple rose at the belief of the night time time.

Esther chose to hold the rose because she modified into so glad with it. She brought it home and located it in a selected vicinity in her mattress room. Since then, Esther has remembered that lovely night time each Valentine's Day via pulling out her rose.

Esther has thinking about knowledgeable limitless human beings about her revel in, demonstrating that Valentine's Day is ready more than actually giving and receiving offers. Esther has in no way forgotten that it is approximately the affection and kindness we show off to every different.

Many individuals had been encouraged thru manner of Esther's narrative at some point of the years, and it's been not unusual to don't forget the birthday celebration night each 3 hundred and sixty five days. Esther can pay tribute to her rose on Valentine's Day thru visiting mainly to the community wherein she initially placed it. She returns to the same location and gets rid of the rose while reflecting on the superb time she had on the Valentine's Day birthday party.

Esther's story serves as a reminder that Valentine's Day is prepared greater than really giving and receiving offers. We want to take the time to particular our gratitude to the ones important people in our life and to motive them to experience loved. Esther's tale serves as evidence that that is the real which means of Valentine's Day.

The Story of Ruth

It is a beautiful tale of herbal love, The Story of Ruth and Valentine's Day. In the Middle Ages, a young girl named Ruth have turn out to be dwelling in a chunk village. Valentine became a wealthy-searching however impoverished guy that she cherished. Ruth made the choice to offer him a wonder present on Valentine's Day. She have turn out to be decided to show him her love and make Valentine's Day specific for him.

To purchase a Valentine's Day gift, Ruth mustered the bravery to go to the marketplace. She provided a solitary rose with the meager amount of money she had. When she arrived to Valentine's home, she gave him the rose.

Chapter 2: The Biblical History Of Valentine's Day

There are numerous numerous property and interpretations that make a contribution to the convoluted and sundry history of Valentine's Day. Some human beings get hold of as true with that the event has its roots within the Roman opposition of Lupercalia, whilst others anticipate it modified into first determined as a Christian night meal honoring the 1/3-century martyr Saint Valentine.

Although Valentine's Day isn't stated within the Bible mainly, many academics think it turn out to be probably inspired through the narrative of Jacob and Rachel in the book of Genesis. In this narrative, Jacob meets Rachel and falls in love at the side of her, however that allows you to get married to her, he have to first art work seven years for her father. A "bouquet of mandrakes" as a symbol of their love is given to Rachel the night time before their wedding ceremony thru Jacob.

Many human beings think the Valentine's Day custom of changing plants and different signs and signs of love is inspired with the aid of this biblical account, that is often seen as a metaphor for the transformative strength of love.

The Bible is complete with verses concerning love, marriage, and relationships similarly to this tale. Jesus tells us inside the New Testament to "love every extraordinary" and "love your neighbor as your self" (John thirteen:34, Matthew 22:39). The apostle Paul exhorts Christians to "love every different with brotherly affection" and to "encourage every different and bring together each different up" (Romans 12:10). (1 Thessalonians 5:eleven).

Valentine's Day, a holiday that celebrates love and relationships, is built on the ideas of those teachings. Although the Bible does now not mainly thing out Valentine's Day, its instructions on love, kindness, and compassion function the muse for the occasion and the customs we even though observe nowadays.

Many Christians assume that Valentine's Day serves as a reminder of God's love for us similarly to a risk to reveal our love for our relationships in addition to our friends and circle of relatives. This is visible in the huge form of Valentine's Day gives that human beings deliver and obtain, together with earrings, vegetation, playing cards, and chocolates in addition to considered one of a kind symptoms and signs of love and affection.

The Bible also exhorts us to "deliver thanks in all times" and to "rejoice in the Lord continually." (Philippians 4:4) (1 Thessalonians 5:18). We ought to take advantage of Valentine's Day to thank humans we like and to renowned all of the advantages God has bestowed upon us.

Valentine's Day is a special event that serves as a reminder of the energy of affection and connections. It is a 2d to hold in mind the price of affection in our lives and to specific gratitude for all of the love we've have been given received, whether or not or now not you're celebrating with a romantic companion, a family member, or a chum.

The importance of self-love, that is something that many humans regularly neglect approximately, is likewise emphasized in the course of the Bible. Healthy relationships are built on the foundation of self-love considering the reality that it's far tough to without a doubt be given and rate the love of others if we do no longer love and take transport of ourselves. We can take benefit of Valentine's Day to practice self-love and to cope with ourselves kindly and compassionately.

Valentine's Day has a huge have an effect on and a robust message, no matter the way you choose out to study it. We ought to preserve and have a good time love on account that it is a crucial component of our lives. Let us therefore be happy for the love we've got in our lifestyles in this Valentine's Day and recollect and honor the biblical teachings on love and relationships.

The biblical command to be content material in our relationships is a few other essential lesson that Valentine's Day serves as a reminder of. Two are main to one, consistent with Ecclesiastes, because they acquire a better recompense for his or her hard art work. Because if one falls, the opportunity is probably picked up. But woe to him who is by way of himself and falls and has no person to help him up! Ecclesiastes four:19–10 This verse serves as a reminder that relationships are vast and that we want to be content material cloth with the people and connections we have were given in our lives. Valentine's Day is an wonderful time to explicit our gratitude for the relationships we have got and to show our appreciation for the people in our lives.

A reminder of God's love for us is provided via Valentine's Day. According to Psalm

103:eleven, God's love is "better than the heavens" and "eternal" (Jeremiah 31:3). Valentine's Day is an brilliant time to don't forget and do not forget God's unwavering love for us and to precise gratitude to Him for His love's advantages.

DEVELOPMENT OF VALENTINE'S DAY

Valentine's Day is an afternoon of birthday party and expression of love determined on February 14th anywhere inside the international. It is difficult to pinpoint the best beginnings of Valentine's Day because of its convoluted statistics. According to a broadly common interpretation, it originated because the pagan birthday celebration of Lupercalia, which turned into located in ancient Rome. Men would probably sacrifice goats and dogs sooner or later of Lupercalia, then whip girls with the hides on the way to boom their fertility.

The Catholic Church made an attempt to convert Valentine's Day from a heathen birthday party to a Christian one inside the

5th century. Legend has it that Saint Valentine become a priest who secretly wed couples in defiance of Emperor Claudius II's orders. When Claudius positioned out approximately this, he had Valentine arrested and later positioned to loss of life. Valentine's Day playing gambling cards are despite the fact that despatched out nowadays due to the truth it's far concept that he left a examine signed "From your Valentine" to his liked earlier than passing away.

Valentine's Day have become a celebrated day for courtly love and romantic gestures within the Middle Ages. As human beings started out changing provides and love letters, the custom of sending greeting cards received recognition. Valentine's Day have emerge as an afternoon of love and passion inside the nineteenth century, and provides of playing cards, goodies, and plant life had been given out to mark the occasion.

Valentine's Day is now an afternoon for showing our love and gratitude to the humans in our lives. Valentine's Day is a time to specific our like to the human beings we care approximately, whether or not it is thru sending a card or a bouquet of plants.

In contemporary years, Valentine's Day has grown in recognition among clients. According to estimates, Americans will spend greater than $20 billion on Valentine's Day in 2021, making it the second one maximum well-known excursion for gift-giving. Additionally, as chocolates, earrings, and one of a type gives are carefully marketed to clients, this tour has grown more commercialized.

Valentine's Day is decided global, at the side of in Japan, in which it's miles known as "White Day" and determined on March 14. On within the meantime, men are anticipated to present ladies with gives like jewelry, plants, or sweets. The 14th of March is likewise Valentine's Day in South Korea, however this holiday is referred to as "Black Day" and is devoted to folks which is probably by myself and who eat black noodles to unique their loneliness.

Valentine's Day is all approximately displaying our loved ones how a good deal we recognize and address them, no matter how it is placed. It's vital to expose our cherished ones how a splendid deal we care, whether or not or no longer it's miles with a honest message or a lavish present.

Around the arena, there are various traditions which can be used to have amusing Valentine's Day. Couples kiss under the mistletoe and trade gives in France, which is probably typically chocolate or vegetation. Couples in Italy commemorate their union with a completely unique supper and present-converting. In the UK, couples frequently watch a romantic film or go out to dinner in addition to converting playing playing cards and flora.

Valentine's Day is now a commonplace day for weddings amongst couples. On Valentine's Day, many couples decide to be married or renew their vows. Additionally, many couples decide to have a Valentine's Day-themed marriage ceremony, complete with decor and song that replicate the day's amorous challenge rely.

How Valentine's Day is a time on the identical time as we are able to display our affection and gratitude for the human beings in our lives and allow them to understand how lots they mean to us.

Chapter 3: Early Christian History Of Valentine's Day

Valentine's Day has been a manner of life for generations and is determined on February 14 each yr. The occasion have become first connected to Christian ideals and changed into celebrated in remembrance of early Christian martyrs.

Valentine, a Roman priest who died as a martyr on February 14th inside the 0.33 century, is credited with making the primary recorded point out of Valentine's Day in his writings. He allegedly officiated at covert marriages for Roman troops who have been prohibited from doing so. The custom of changing playing playing playing cards and gives on Valentine's Day commenced out even as he wrote a word signed "From your Valentine" to a younger woman he had turn out to be friends with.

In 496 AD, the Catholic Church officially embraced the birthday party and named it in honor of St. Valentine. People began replacing gambling playing playing cards and offers in honor of St. Valentine within the route of the Middle Ages even as it became a well-known occasion. The birthday celebration had modified with the resource of the 1400s to include all sorts of amorous gestures, such bringing vegetation and candies.

The Puritans in England and America antagonistic the competition and forbade it within the 17th century, but it became in the end resurrected in both countries in the 19th century. Valentine's Day is now a extensively determined vacation in each u . S . A .. It is an afternoon to express your love and gratitude in your family, which includes your associate, pals, and family.

Valentine's Day has often turn out to be a secular birthday party in modern times, however it although has deep origins in early Christian facts. On February 14, numerous church houses host specific services and celebrations. In addition to sexual relationships, different sorts of relationships and familial ties within the suggest time are blanketed within the party of affection and resolution.

Valentine's Day has superior into an afternoon to provide thank you for the people in our life, display our love for the ones we do, and don't forget how crucial healthy relationships are. Regardless of the manner the holiday is determined, it serves as a crucial reminder of the power of love and the fee of cherishing the people we care about.

Although Valentine's Day's data has changed at some point of the years, its early Christian origins have remained firmly entrenched. The opposition maintains to function a reminder of the significance of displaying our cherished ones appreciation, although it has been more secularized over the years.

On February 14th, many people use the opportunity to honor their relationships via sending playing playing cards and items to their loved ones. It's an afternoon to keep in thoughts the price of relationships with buddies, family, and romantic companions. In order to interact with their corporations and inspire people to make the effort to comprehend their relationships and precise their gratitude to the ones they care approximately, many church homes and different religion-based totally corporations employ Valentine's Day as an event.

The 0.33 century and the martyrdom of St. Valentine are while the Christian subculture of Valentine's Day first emerged. The electricity of love is established thru his instance of selflessness and self-discipline to others. We will pay homage to this records on Valentine's Day thru being type and loving to folks who are close to us.

Early Christian Traditions

Valentine's Day customs originated within the early Christian era and date lower back to the 0.33 century. The day is concept to have started out as a celebration in memory of Saint Valentine, a Roman Catholic priest who modified into killed for his piety. The day come to be supposedly discovered through giving flora, playing playing playing cards, and different expressions of affection to people in need.

Valentine's Day modified right into a romantic and absolutely glad excursion in the Middle Ages. Flowers, paper playing cards, and candies were common gadgets given and bought. They also can alternate love poems and messages. People however take a look at the ones customs in a few regions of the location when they have an excellent time for the time being.

Valentine's Day is a public tour inside the United States. Couples trade devices and playing cards in this day, and often romantic dinners and different forms of amusement are included. On this modern-day, severa colleges, church homes, and corporations also host unique activities.

St. Valentine have turn out to be seen as a martyr for his beliefs, which served as the foundation for the early Christian customs surrounding Valentine's Day. The event however has Christian roots, however modern-day shift towards a extra secular party. People notwithstanding the reality that undergo in mind the love and sacrifice St. Valentine made for his religion and commemorate him.

Valentine's Day is a day to have an exquisite time and display our loved ones how lots we admire them. Gifts like playing cards, chocolates, and vegetation are frequently given as gives to friends, circle of relatives, and remarkable loved ones. Others need to spend wonderful time together, collectively with by means of using manner of going to a film or consuming supper out. Romantic gestures like mailing love letters or sincere messages are also frequently exchanged. Many individuals supply their friends, loved ones, and large others gives on Valentine's Day to expose how plenty they care.

Valentine's Day is a day to famend the fee of friendship as well as to have a outstanding time love. By making small efforts like sending a card or bringing a chum to lunch, many humans take some time to connect with their buddies and show them that they care. Spending time with own family and expressing your gratitude to them is any other custom.

The vacation of Valentine's Day honors friendship and love. Valentine's Day has grown into a mundane birthday party of love and appreciation on the equal time as keeping its early Christian customs. The excursion season is a time whilst many people spend time considering the price of friendship and expressing their love and gratitude to the ones closest to them.

The day of love and kindness has additionally superior into Valentine's Day. To generate coins for humans in need, an entire lot of agencies preserve philanthropic sports activities and fundraisers. People additionally regularly supply to reasons which are pricey to their hearts. For instance, humans may want to likely deliver to agencies that useful useful resource folks that are hungry, homeless, or in need of scientific interest.

Valentine's Day moreover serves as a time for people to honor the ones who've passed away. In order to recognize their reminiscence, human beings often pay visits to the graves of loved ones and leave flora or cards. Some human beings additionally use the time to reconnect with pals and family they haven't seen in some time as they spend the day thinking about how critical love and friendship are.

Valentine's Day is a widespread event that honors friendship, charity, and love. Many human beings use the day to bear in mind people who are luxurious to them, and the day's early Christian customs are although practiced in recent times. People exhibit their love and gratitude for the ones round them via imparting provides, making charitable contributions, and spending time with friends and own family.

Medieval Legends

Valentine's Day, everyday with a famous medieval delusion, has its start with a Catholic priest named Saint Valentine who lived in Rome within the zero.33 century. In retaining with the myth that unmarried men make better soldiers, Emperor Claudius II forbade more youthful men from getting married. Valentine disobeyed the emperor and discreetly wed couples who have been deeply in love. Eventually, he became apprehended and given the dying penalty. Prior to being located to death, he despatched a letter to the jailer's daughter and signed it "from your Valentine."

Valentine come to be allegedly imprisoned, in keeping with every other model, for supporting Christians in escaping from Roman jails. He reportedly treated his jailer's daughter on the identical time as he modified into internal and despatched her a letter wherein he professed his love for her. This metropolis legend, which has turn out to be related with Valentine's Day, is referred to as justification for the card- and present-converting customs decided in this occasion.

The tale of the birds is the maximum famous Valentine's Day tale. The birds might also begin to couple off on February 14th, everyday with mythology, in schooling for mating season. This changed into interpreted as a signal of clean love, and it have grow to be venerated with gambling cards and provides.

Whichever of these myths is real, it's far simple that Valentine's Day has a prolonged records. It has been celebrated for generations, and there can be no indication that it will prevent any time brief.

The martyrdom of Saint Valentine is a special Valentine's Day legend. In accordance with this legend, Valentine changed into executed as a martyr for his steadfast adherence to Christianity. Many should honor his sacrifice with the useful resource of sending him playing cards and flora at the day of the anniversary of his beheading.

The historical Roman pageant of Lupercalia and Valentine's Day are associated. This occasion venerated fertility and feature emerge as held in February. Men could choose names at random from slips of paper that women had written their names on. This would be the companion they could have for the entire 365 days.

Since Valentine's Day has been decided for see you later, many nations now consider it to be a significant excursion. It is a day to honor affection, friendship, and ties to others. Valentine's Day is a cute birthday party this is guaranteed to unfold joy and like to many, whether or not you pick out out out to honor the legends or just experience the day with a person unique.

Another issue that makes Valentine's Day famous is its connection to courtly love. Courtiers often wrote or sent gadgets to their loved ones on Valentine's Day inside the path of the Middle Ages. This custom has been persevered into the modern-day-day, even as humans regularly ship playing gambling cards, chocolates, and unique offers to expose their love.

The "Birds of Love" story is likewise related to Valentine's Day. This myth states that on the eve of Valentine's Day, birds ought to bounce over houses of couples and utter heartfelt messages of love. This custom has been practiced at some point of a large variety of cultural contexts and is a loved hassle of the holiday.

People frequently reaffirm their love for each exceptional and have a good time it on Valentine's Day. Valentine's Day is a adorable birthday celebration this is guaranteed to spread joy and like to many, whether or now not or now not you pick out to honor the legends or truly enjoy the day with someone specific.

Early Church Fathers

Valentine's Day has a extended and complicated beyond, with its origins within the early Roman technology. Valentine modified into the call of two martyrs who have been venerated on February 14th, making them the earliest Church Fathers related to the vacation.

The first Valentine grow to be a Roman priest who died a martyr's death in 269 under the guideline of thumb of Emperor Claudius II. He become detained for marrying younger troops that the monarch had forbade from getting married. He received an execution verdict as a stop quit end result. He won notoriety at the same time as he became imprisoned for his selfless deeds of charity, which blanketed curing the jailer's daughter of her blindness. In addition to being the consumer saint of affection, teenagers, and rich marriages, he is famend for his bravery and kindness.

The second Valentine became an Italian bishop from Terni who died as a martyr within the year 375. He is idea to had been achieved with the aid of beheading in protest of the Roman Emperor's persecution of Christians. His devoted issuer to the Terni humans is what makes him synonymous with the concept of courtly love.

Valentine's Day is a worldwide life-style this is intrinsically associated with the legacies of those Church Fathers. On nowadays, we ought to commemorate the ones martyrs' bravery and devotion even as additionally celebrating love and charity.

Exchanging playing cards, giving items, and spending time with cherished ones are only some of the sports that now make up the modern-day-day Valentine's Day birthday party. In many additives of the arena, the event has grow to be commercialized, with people shopping for plant life, goodies, and other gives for their cherished ones. The legacy of the two Church Fathers who served as the holiday's concept and its historic context need to but be remembered.

The cause of Valentine's Day is to honor the ones martyrs' bravery and commitment at the same time as moreover celebrating love and goodwill. It's a time to unique our gratitude to the people we care approximately and to be appreciative for them. Additionally, it's miles a day to mirror on the selfless deeds of kindness that the 2 Church Fathers completed for others and to clear up to act with the identical degree of compassion and generosity in our personal lives.

The Church Fathers' legacies are remembered and venerated on Valentine's Day in various cultures. To hear memories approximately the lives and deeds of affection of these martyrs, human beings regularly gather for services of their network church homes. Valentine's Day banquets, dances, and parades are some examples of the precise occasions and sports activities which may be typically held to mark the event.

Valentine's Day is a time to consider the compassion and love that the 2 Church Fathers displayed closer to others and to take the time to live our lives in a manner that exemplifies those same capabilities. It is likewise a day to specific our affection and gratitude for the manual and love that we get hold of from the people we care about.

No count number range our method of Valentine's Day birthday celebration, it's far critical to keep in mind the two Church Fathers who served as its perception and to appreciate their legacy. Their reminiscences characteristic a reminder that compassion and love can be triumphant even the maximum trying situations and that our surroundings may be significantly impacted by way of way of our deeds of kindness.

Chapter 4: Medieval History Of Valentine's Day

The origins of Valentine's Day may be located in medieval Europe, irrespective of the fact that it can seem like a cutting-edge-day celebration of affection. St. Valentine grow to be a Catholic saint who lived in Rome inside the 0.33 century, and his dinner party day modified into related to Valentine's Day at some point of the Middle Ages. On February 14, human beings can also commemorate St. Valentine's Day through way of giving offers to their loved ones. It changed into idea that he had the strength to heal people.

In addition, it modified into notion that birds commenced out mating on February 14; that is why Valentine's Day is widely known on that day. Because of this, it have become regular for couples to jot down a similarly love letters and greeting cards, a custom this is however mounted nowadays.

A purple rose turned into traditionally visible as a photo of love in the Middle Ages, and those may placed on or provide them to others. This concept in all likelihood originated with the Roman goddess Juno, who turn out to be associated with fertility and marriage. As a conventional Valentine's Day present, pink roses are in spite of the truth that often supplied.

In the ancient Roman Lupercalia competition, Valentine's Day moreover has its origins. This mid-February party venerated the fertility god and have become held at that factor.

It grow to be no longer till the Middle Ages that Valentine's Day commenced out to benefit popularity. People may also exchange affords and verbally speak their thoughts to each other ultimately of this time to show their affection for every other. A man and woman retaining their love for each other on Valentine's Day have been moreover idea to have perfect good fortune in love for the the rest of the 12 months in a few areas.

Additionally, inside the direction of this time period, Valentine's Day card and letter-writing customs had been set up. These gambling cards were in the beginning composed of parchment and embellished with romantic symbols and plant life. In normally, a wax seal became used to seal them. The majority of Valentine's Day playing cards in recent times are composed of paper and embellished with hearts, ribbons, and cupids.

Giving flowers on Valentine's Day commenced out out to benefit popularity in the Middle Ages as well. Even in recent times, people however gift purple roses as tokens of their love due to the fact they have been previously notion to be a picture of that emotion. On Valentine's Day, carnations, daisies, and lilies are also often given as plant life.

Valentine's Day has modified over time, however its origins in the Middle Ages are despite the fact that apparent nowadays. To display their love for a person, human beings though offer gives, deliver playing playing cards and plants, and trade presents.

Furthermore, the medieval custom of courtly love is attached to Valentine's Day. It modified into considered suitable to understand and honor this unique sort of love that existed among nobility participants. In some cultures, it come to be regular for someone to provide a gift to a girl in remembrance of their shared courtly affection. This gift might be a Valentine's Day card or a group of flowers.

The Middle Ages observed a boom in numerous superstitions collectively with the observance of Valentine's Day. On Valentine's Day, it became belief that if a female located a robin flying overhead, she would wed a sailor, even as if she noticed a sparrow, she might wed a horrific man however be very content material.

Valentine's Day stays discovered and honored for its medieval historical beyond these days. People though supply purple roses as a image of affection on Valentine's Day in addition to changing playing cards and affords. The essence of Valentine's Day hasn't changed in spite of the bulk of the Middle Ages' customs and superstitions having been abandoned.

MODERN HISTORY OF VALENTINE'S DAY

Since the Middle Ages, people have loved celebrating Valentine's Day, that is commonly determined on February 14. To honor the Christian martyr St. Valentine, it changed into first off a religious excursion. The occasion has superior into an earthly birthday party of friendship and love over time.

Valentine's Day commenced out to be openly determined and become increasingly linked to romantic love within the 18th century. Valentine's Day playing gambling playing cards have been exchanged during this time, generally adorned with lace and plant life. Valentine's Day gambling gambling cards became a not unusual present for cherished ones by the early 19th century due to the fact to mass manufacture.

Valentine's Day became heavily marketed within the 20th century, and the traditional gambling playing cards had been modified with the aid of extra modern-day-day offers like goodies, jewelry, and filled animals. In the twenty-first century, this pattern persisted, and Valentine's Day has thinking about grown to be a multi-billion greenback enterprise.

Valentine's Day is now a properly diagnosed vacation this is observed all around the global as a manner of displaying appreciation and love. Even even though it is although largely a romantic occasion, Valentine's Day is likewise a time to show your family how lots you care. Along with the greater traditional gives, gift playing playing playing cards, spa applications, and studies are some of the most nicely-favored modern-day Valentine's Day offers.

Also at some stage in time, Valentine's Day has broadened in scope. Today, it is also an afternoon to honor platonic love, self-love, and love for all different styles of relationships. Valentine's Day isn't best a day to have fun romantic love. The LGBT community has additionally decided methods to personalize Valentine's Day, with loads of activities and festivities catered to the institution.

Additionally, Valentine's Day has developed to be an awful lot extra available to human beings from all particular monetary situations. Everybody can now discover a present that conveys their love and appreciation way to the abundance of less expensive gadgets to be had online and in shops. From the start of Valentine's Day, whilst gambling playing cards and offers were often highly-priced and out of many people's charge tiers, this has changed considerably.

From its non secular origins in the Middle Ages, Valentine's Day has lengthy past an extended manner. People from all backgrounds commemorate this contemporary, which has grown to be immensely famous, as a time to honor love in all of its manifestations.

As a long way as how it's far honored, Valentine's Day has moreover modified. Despite the continuing recognition of the standard gambling cards and gives, human beings now moreover have fun with romantic dinners, romantic vacations, and different activities that entail spending wonderful time with their cherished ones. Due to the instant functionality to deliver messages of love and gratitude round the sector, the internet and social media have also altered how people have fun.

In phrases of the humans with whom it's miles celebrated, Valentine's Day has accelerated in contemporary day years. Now, further to celebrating high-quality others, it is an afternoon to precise gratitude to shut friends, family contributors, and even pets. Valentine's Day is now not pretty much romantic love, as it as quickly as grow to be.

From its early Middle Ages beginnings, Valentine's Day has long long past an extended way. People from many backgrounds have fun it because it has grown to be a famous excursion that honors love in all its manifestations. Valentine's Day is the first-class opportunity to explicit your love for the unique humans in your lifestyles, whether or no longer you're celebrating with a massive other, a friend, a member of the family, or a doggy.

Chapter 5: Ancient Roman Customs And Traditions

The hard machine of traditions and customs practiced via way of the Ancient Romans has grown to be important to their way of lifestyles. These traditions were created over a few years and handed down from father to son.

Roman pageant calendar turn out to be one exquisite custom. The Romans located a exceptional festival every month to commemorate large sports activities of their information or to honor a specific deity. Religious rituals, consuming, and public competitions had been frequently held together with those celebrations.

The Roman approach of burial come to be each different vast dependancy. Usually, the departed have been laid to rest in a tomb or mausoleum that housed a marble or stone slab with an inscription in their honor. These graves had been frequently adorned with sculptures and paintings that portrayed the deceased's existence and accomplishments.

Superstition modified into a powerful force in Roman tradition, too. They believed that with the beneficial useful resource of sporting out particular rites, horrific success will be prevented if it befell a person. For example, to fend off ill desirable fortune, one may throw a handful of salt over their shoulder earlier than crossing a threshold.

The Romans of antiquity carried out a exquisite role in every literature and artwork. They created works of paintings similar to the statues of gods and goddesses as well as epic poetry similar to the Aeneid and the Odyssey. Romans also valued theater and drama relatively, and their theaters have been regularly ornate houses with seating for a big amount of viewers.

Roman social lifestyles become likewise dominated with the aid of their traditions and conventions. They had been stated for their heat hospitality, and it became not unusual exercise to offer meals and wine as a form of greeting. They also enjoyed going to public baths and attending occasions like gladiatorial fights.

Additionally, the Romans of antiquity valued circle of relatives lifestyles appreciably. Roman culture positioned a excessive price on marriage, and families frequently helped installation unions. Women were predicted to live right to their husbands, and if they had been observed to be untrue, they faced punishment.

They have been deeply rooted in the historical Roman traditions and practices. The traditions and way of existence of contemporary-day Italy though reflect them.

Lupercalia

A festival known as Lupercalia have come to be held in the early to mid-February in historic Rome. It come to be devoted to the god Faunus, who guarded shepherds and their flocks and grow to be allied with

Lupercus, the fertility god. The 3-day opposition become typically marked thru a number of rituals and ceremonies, in conjunction with animal sacrifices, fertility rites, and ceremonial purification.

Two extra younger guys had been decided on to represent Lupercus and had been given goatskin thongs on the number one day of Lupercalia (known as februa). They were then introduced to the Lupercal, a respected grotto on the Palatine Hill wherein it's far believed that the she-wolf nursed the legendary founders of Rome, Romulus and Remus. Here, a goat and a dog were slain via the priests of Lupercus, and after that, the blood from the animals modified into used to anoint the two more youthful guys. Then, because the men went at some stage in the Palatine Hill, they used the februa to attack everybody they came across. This have come to be done with the want that it might enhance every the health and fertility of every human beings and animals.

Throughout Lupercalia, a second ceremony took place. The two young guys used the februa to gently strike the Roman ladies who have been gathered in a line along the streets. This changed into idea to bestow fertility and prosperity upon the women. The younger guys then engaged in a traditional dinner party that featured milk and honey after the ceremony, during which they slaughtered a sheep.

In the fifth century, the Christian excursion of Candlemas step by step took the place of the Lupercalian festival. Some of the competition's customs and traditions, appreciably those pertaining to fertility and fitness, are nevertheless practiced these days.

Lupercalia come to be visible as a massive duration for cleansing and purification similarly to fertility and fitness. The februatio ritual turn out to be accomplished at the competition's remaining day. A canine had to be sacrificed for this, and after it have become skinned, the hide needed to be divided into strips. These strips were then gently whipped by means of members after being soaked within the blood of the sacrifice. People were purified and cleansed of any terrible power or sick top fortune consistent with this tool.

The Lupercalia opposition played a brilliant position in the development of historic Roman way of existence and traditions, and it is though discovered in a few form nowadays. It stays seen as a season of regeneration and sparkling beginnings and is associated with fertility, fitness, purification, and cleansing.

The Origin of the Holiday

Valentine's Day is a completely precise occasion for humans to precise their love and gratitude for each one-of-a-kind. The occasion is thought to have began out in ancient Rome, but its real beginnings are in maximum instances uncertain. During this time, a pageant modified into held in honor of Lupercus, the Roman god of fertility. Young males and females would congregate within the town's streets at some stage in this pageant, which grow to be observed on February 15th, and draw plenty to determine who might be their companions for the celebration.

The birthday party protected ingesting, creating a music, and dancing, and participants were suggested to offer their companions with gadgets. A home made paper Valentine become the most significantly used present. Typically, the ones Valentines have been decorated with plants, ribbons, and exclusive love-associated devices.

The historic Roman competition modified into determined with the sacrifice of a goat and a canine similarly to the giving and receiving of Valentine gambling cards. These creatures have been revered due to the reality the divine keepers of fertility and love. Strips of their hides had been reduce after the sacrifice and used to shape a whip. Then, that lets in you to increase their fertility, more youthful men have to lash girls within the streets.

Although the vintage Roman competition is not decided, fantastic of its customs are even though observed in contemporary Valentine's Day. People now deliver and get maintain of playing playing playing cards, vegetation, and one-of-a-kind romantic objects. Kissing has taken the placement of the whipping ritual and is stated to convey couples fulfillment and happiness.

It is apparent that Valentine's Day has its roots in historical Roman rituals and traditions, regardless of the way you choose to have fun it. Therefore, pause for a second to don't forget the significance of this specific day and make certain to specific your love and gratitude to dad and mom which can be close to you.

Red and white are the traditional solar sunglasses associated with Valentine's Day. White represents innocence and purity, while red stands for ardour and love. The bride wore a white veil, and the groom usually wore a pink tunic, therefore those shades had been in all likelihood selected to symbolize the common Roman bridal ceremony customs.

Another well-known Valentine's Day brand is the coronary heart. This emblem dates decrease again to the Roman generation, whilst Jupiter, the god of affection, have end up symbolized via way of the heart. The coronary heart form superior right into a famous example of love and romance through the years.

Another custom that originated in ancient Rome is the giving and receiving of objects on Valentine's Day. People used to change modest devices of love again then, which includes flowers, jewels, and candies. These same types of affords are in spite of the fact that well-known these days, but they could moreover encompass goodies, toy animals, and greeting playing cards.

It is apparent that Valentine's Day has its roots in ancient Roman rituals and traditions, regardless of how you pick out to check the event. Therefore, pause for a 2d to hold in mind the importance of this particular day and make sure to explicit your love and gratitude to parents which are close to you.

Chapter 6: Modern Celebrations Of Valentine's Day

Every yr on February 14th, people everywhere inside the international commemorate Valentine's Day as a totally unique occasion. It is unsure in which it came from, but it is belief to have began as a way to honor the Christian saint Valentine inside the Roman Empire.

Depending on the manner of life and traditions of the celebrants, Valentine's Day is now determined in a number of techniques. Giving playing cards, converting items, and wearing crimson are only some of the customs which are well-known nowadays. Other sports can consist of taking a romantic retreat, seeing a romantic movie, or going out for a unique dinner.

Valentine's Day is a famous day for giving devices, and the most common gives are candies, flowers, jewelry, and luxurious animals. A romantic poem or an occasion, consisting of a heat air balloon flight or a spa day, are some unusual offers that people can pick out to provide.

The manner that human beings test Valentine's Day has moreover altered because of era. Valentine's Day-associated content material is plentiful on famous net structures like TikTok, YouTube, and Instagram, and it tiers from DIY gift mind to sappy video messages. Another great approach to choice your own family a satisfied Valentine's Day is through social media.

The most important element about Valentine's Day is that it is a completely unique day to have amusing love and appreciation for the ones we care about, regardless of how human beings pick out out to have an great time it.

Valentine's Day Cards

Valentine's Day playing playing cards are a fantastic manner to unique your love and gratitude for a particular someone. There are such a lot of particular types of playing

playing cards to select out out from, beginning from sincere and endearing vows to passionate and romantic ones. These gambling cards are the perfect manner to express your love, whether or not you want to mention "I love you" or "Happy Valentine's Day."

A form of substances, which include paper, cloth, felt, or maybe timber, can be used to create Valentine's Day gambling playing cards. To make a few gambling cards greater super, glitter, ribbons, and rhinestones are introduced to them. Some playing playing playing cards are even extra one-of-a-type and extremely good because they've got a particular backdrop image or message.

Consider the character, hobbies, and alternatives of the recipient at the same time as deciding on Valentine's Day playing cards. Consider a card with cartoon characters or ambitious hues if it's far for a kid, as an instance. Choose a greater conventional and sensitive layout in case you are gifting the cardboard to a more mature recipient.

Regardless of the kind of Valentine's Day card you pick out, it's going to absolutely make the receiver revel in valued and unique. These gambling cards, which variety from lighter, humorous sentiments to passionate confessions of affection, will display screen your state of affairs for the recipient.

Cards for Valentine's Day are also a remarkable manner to specific gratitude to those who have supported you at some degree inside the 12 months. These cards are a heartfelt manner to precise gratitude to a person, whether or not or now not or now not it's a determine, sibling, friend, or coworker. You can select a card that expresses your sentiments and mind or even personalize it to make it more massive.

Cards on Valentine's Day are also excellent offers. These gambling playing cards will supply your affection to someone, whether you're romantically involved with them or they'll be first-rate a completely unique a part of your lifestyles. You have the choice of choosing a card that conveys your emotions of affection and gratitude for them or collectively with a customized be conscious to the card.

Whatever style of Valentine's Day card you select, it will absolutely be valued and precious for future years. Don't overlook to supply the perfect card to your loved ones on Valentine's Day to expose them how masses you care.

Gifts and Flowers

Valentine's Day is a fantastic event for showing our loved ones how a whole lot we apprehend them. It's a day whole of love, happiness, and gives. Flowers are a number of the most notably used offers on Valentine's Day.

Giving someone plants is a traditional manner to reveal them which you care. Some of the maximum properly-desired Valentine's Day flower arrangements are tulips, lilies, and roses. Red roses are mainly properly-favored for the cause that they stand for passion and love. Carnations and daisies are other not unusual flower types.

On Valentine's Day, some of humans moreover deliver chocolates and unique affords in addition to flora. Chocolates are a delicious manner to unique your love. Gifts like earrings and cuddly animals are also commonplace. Create a completely unique gift basket filled with matters that your unique a person will like if you're looking for a few difficulty more intimate.

Valentine's Day is the proper event to specific your need to a person. Don't forget to reveal your love and gratitude for the important humans for your lifestyles with a thoughtful message or an association of plants.

Valentine's Day is a well-desired day for fanatics to provide and gather presents from each specific. Jewelry, watches, garments, and one-of-a-kind gadgets that express how masses they value every other are famous amongst couples. There are many customised gives to be had for people attempting to find a few problem extra wonderful. There are many strategies to precise your love to your exquisite exclusive, from customized mugs to photograph albums.

Valentine's Day is a very precise event to reveal your love and gratitude. Show the special humans in your existence how loads you care with a present, whether or now not it is a personalized object, rings, flora, or goodies.

Chapter 7: Valentine's Day Comes Annually

Across the us and in first-rate regions all around the earth, chocolates, plants, and gives are transferred among pals and own family, worried approximately the reason of St. Valentine. Yet, who is this difficult holy person and in which did the ones rituals originate from? Learn about the means and history of Valentine's Day, from the ancient Roman festival of Lupercalia that welcomed spring to the card-giving customs of Victorian Britain.

The Legend of St. Valentine

Holy character Valentine, who as suggested via numerous opinions is genuinely precise, installed characters who were stated to have recuperated a youngster even as arrested and killed thru the use of beheading.

Where did Valentine's Day come from?

The records of the competition — and the story of its assisting holy man or woman — is hidden in secrecy. We honestly do understand that February has for pretty some time been lauded as a month of feeling and that St. Valentine's Day, as an extended way as we is probably worried nowadays, has elements of each Christian and archaic Roman lifestyle. In any case, which have become the Holy character Valentine, and the way might also want to he emerge as related to this ancient ritual?

The Catholic Church identifies no fewer than three separate saintly individuals referred to as Valentine or Valentinus, and every considered certainly one of them have become martyred. One tale contends that Valentine become a minister who served throughout the third a hundred years in Rome.

At the point at the same time as Ruler Claudius II concluded that lonely guys had been better officers than people with marriages and kids, he forbade marriage for younger fellows. Valentine, figuring out the injustice of the announcement, disputed Claudius and persevered on executing connections for greater youthful darlings surreptitiously.

At the time while Valentine's moves were uncovered, Claudius asked that he be slain. Still, others insist that it changed into Holy Saint Valentine of Terni, a diocesan, who became the actual namesake of the event. He, likewise, changed into killed with the useful aid of Claudius II outside Rome.

Different legends provide that Valentine may additionally moreover have been assassinated for looking to assist Christians with escaping break out from harsh Roman penitentiaries, wherein they have been routinely assaulted and tormented. As consistent with one narrative, a jailed Valentine actually despatched the first "valentine" welcome himself after he went crazy over a younger baby — probable his jailor's daughter — who visited him in a few unspecified time inside the destiny of his captivity. Before his dying, it's far believed that he maintained contact along with her with a letter endorsing "From your Valentine," an articulation this is though getting used nowadays.

Albeit the reality underlying the Valentine memories is dubious, the stories all spotlight his appeal as a thoughtful, chivalrous, and - specially — emotional guy. By the Medieval Ages, probable due to this recognition, Valentine ought to turn out to be pretty probable the maximum famend non secular man or woman in Britain and France.

Starting elements of Valentine's Day:

An Agnostic Celebration in February

While a few accumulate that Valentine's Day is counseled in February to honor the commemoration of Valentine's passing or entombment — which maximum possibly happened round A.D. 270 — others guarantee that the Christian church may want to in all likelihood have decided directly to area St.

Valentine's gala day in February with an cease goal to "Christianize" the agnostic festival of Lupercalia. Celebrated at some stage in the ides of February, or February 15, Lupercalia grow to be a fruitfulness competition devoted to Faunus, the Roman lord of horticulture, as nicely with recognize to the Roman pioneers Romulus and Remus.

To start the birthday celebration, humans from the Luperci, a request for Roman ministers, might also want to collect in a sacred grotto in which the babies Romulus and Remus, the pioneers within the again of Rome, had been stated to had been definitely targeted on with the useful resource of a she-wolf or lupa. The ministers have to sacrifice a goat, for adulthood, and a dog, for sanitization.

They need to then shred the goat's stow away into strips, dip them into the conciliatory blood, and insurrection, tenderly slapping the two girls and harvest fields with the goat stow away.

A lengthy manner from being unlucky, Roman girls invited the hint of the stows away considering making them greater prolific in the approaching three hundred and sixty five days become stylish. Later within the day, as regular with legend, each one of the young girls inside the town might also positioned their names in a chief urn.

The city's unmarried person grownup men should every select a call and get partnered for the 3 hundred and sixty five days together together with his favored female. These relationships typically culminated in marriage.

Valentine's Day Meaning:

A Day of Sentiment and Love

Lupercalia withstood the underlying ascension of Christianity, but, turned into forbidden — as it end up appeared "un-Christian" — close to the stop of the 5th hundred years, at the equal time as Pope Gelasius proclaimed February 14 St. Valentine's Day. It become in reality loads later, regardless of the truth that, that the day had been given definitively related to devotion.

During the Medieval Ages, it changed into usually relied on in France and Britain that February 14 became the start of birds' mating season, which prompted the ability that the center of Valentine's Day desires to be an afternoon for emotion. The English author Geoffrey Chaucer turn out to be brief to describe St.

Valentine's Day as an afternoon of emotional satisfaction in his 1375 sonnet "Parliament of Fouls," announcing, "For this modified into despatched on Saint Valentine's Day/When every foul cometh there to choose his partner."

Valentine's superb tidings had been broadly referred to as lengthy decrease again because the Medieval Ages, yet composed Valentine's did now not start to reveal up until approximately 1400.

The most stated found out valentine final in life these days modified right into a sonnet composed in 1415 via using Charles, Duke of Orleans, to his widespread particular even as he changed into incarcerated within the Pinnacle of London after his capture on the Clash of Agincourt.

(The properly day is now critical for the genuine replica collection of the English Library in London, Britain.) Quite a long time later, it's miles mentioned that Ruler Henry V engaged an essayist known as John Lydgate to compose a valentine's message to Catherine of Valois.

Who Is Cupid?

Cupid is generally represented on Valentine's Day playing cards as an uncovered seraph capturing out bolts of devotion at unsuspecting sweethearts. Be that as it can, the Roman God Cupid has his roots in Greek legend because the Greek heavenly electricity of devotion, Eros.

Records of his the front to the universe variety; some claim he is the offspring of Nyx and Erebus; others, of Aphrodite and Ares; but some take delivery of as proper with he's the child of Iris and Zephyrus or perhaps Aphrodite and Zeus (who also can have been the 2 his dad and grandpa) (who might have been the two his dad and granddad).

As indicated by means of manner of the Greek Old-ordinary authors, Eros have come to be an attractive unfading toyed with the feelings of Divine beings and mortals, employing mind-blowing bolts to bring about love and hefty ones to plant repugnance.

It changed into best during the Greek generation that he got here to be demonstrated due to the fact the wicked, obese boy he'd grow to be on Valentine's Day playing playing cards.

Run-of-the-mill Valentine's Day Good tidings and Gifts

Notwithstanding the united states, Valentine's Day is cited in Canada, Mexico, the Assembled Realm, France, and Australia. In Extraordinary England, Valentine's Day commenced out to be actively located about the seventeenth a hundred years.

By the middle of the eighteenth, it modified into normal for pals and lovers of all amicable instructions to trade tiny badges of affection or transcribed notes, and by using using 1900 determined gambling cards began to alternative written letters because of improvements in printing innovation.

Instant playing cards had been an easy manner for parents to percentage their emotions whilst the direct articulation of 1's perspectives have come to be prevented. Less pricey postal expenses likewise added about an expansion in the recognition of mailing Valentine's Day fantastic tidings.

Americans possibly started out out sharing hand-made valentines in the mid-1700s. During the 1840s, Esther A. Howland started out selling the primary effectively produced valentines in America.

Howland, regarded due to the fact the "Mother of the Valentine," lengthy-established hard representations with proper trim, strips, and exquisite drawings referred to as "scrap." Today, as discovered out by way of the Hello Card Affiliation, an anticipated a hundred forty five million Valentine's Day gambling cards are sent each twelve months, making Valentine's Heart with satisfaction the second one finest card-sending occasion of the only year (extra gambling playing cards are sent at Christmas) (more gambling playing cards are despatched at Christmas).

What's more, how may moreover want to he remodel into the unofficial mascot of Valentine's Day?

The image of Cupid in the important invokes thoughts of a cherubic teenager utilizing a bow and bolt; however, this wasn't generally the case. Well earlier than the Romans observed and renamed him — and an prolonged manner earlier than his hyperlink with Valentine's Day — Cupid have become diagnosed through the Greeks as Eros, the beautiful heavenly electricity of devotion.

Cupid and Greek Folklore

Quite in all likelihood the primary writer to make factor out of Eros (about seven-hundred B.C.) changed into Hesiod, who represented him in "Theogony" as one of the primal cosmogonic divinities delivered into the world of the sector egg.

Be that as it could, next reviews of the heredity of Eros variety, depicting him due to the fact the offspring of Nyx and Erebus; Aphrodite and Ares; or Iris and Zephyrus; or maybe Aphrodite and Zeus — who may additionally moreover were the 2 his dad and grandpa.

Furnished with a bow and a quiver stocked up with each brilliant bolts to stir choice and weighty bolts to kindle revolution, Eros struck at the hearts of celestial creatures and mortals and toyed with their sentiments.

In one account from historic Greek legend, which was subsequently repeated by the use of manner of Roman authors, Cupid (Eros) threw a shocking bolt at Apollo, who have become wildly smitten with the fairy Daphne, but, at that point positioned out a hefty bolt at Daphne so she might be repulsed by way of using him.

Cupid and Mind

In every other planned legend, Cupid's mum, Venus (Aphrodite), grew to emerge as out to be so jealous of the fantastic human Mind that she encouraged her infant to push Mind to transport crazy for a beast.

All things being equal, Cupid have become as heaps as be so enthusiastic about the resource of Mind that he married her — at the condition that she might in no manner see his face.

At remaining, Mind's fascination have been given the higher of her and she or he or he took a peek, making Cupid flee out of contamination. Subsequent to travelling the nicely-found additives of the globe seeking out her lover, Mind have grow to be ultimately reconnected with Cupid and licensed the present of eternality.

In the lyric of the Obsolete time period, Eros have become addressed as a hunky everlasting who modified into overwhelming to each man and celestial entities. In any occasion, in the course of the Greek generation, he come to be an increasing number of represented as a a laugh-loving, mischievous youngster. Due to his link with love, nineteenth-century Victorians — credited with promoting Valentine's Day and giving the occasion its emotional touch — began providing this cherubic shape of Cupid on Valentine's Day cards in a sample that has remained till this current.

Chapter 8: Vinegar Valentines Went From Cheeky To Brutal

Before they have been termed vinegar valentines, the ones irreverent cards have been called taunting or comic valentines. Their tone superior from a diffused punch to out-and-out forcefulness.

There changed into an insulting card for nearly each person someone should possibly loathe — from bothersome salespeople and landlords to repressive employers and foes of severa types. Cards is probably mailed off liars and cheaters and teases and drunkards, on the identical time as specific cards taunted specific vocations.

Their notable snap shots embodied traditional preconceptions and insulted a beneficiary's right attributes, lack of a marital companion, or character competencies.

Suffragettes received focus while the ladies' testimony increase accrued up momentum. "The gambling playing cards usually brought up ethical downfalls. Maybe it have become depended on at times that they may result in an adjustment of conduct, but usually speakme their aim become basically to admonish or perhaps to injure," says Dust.

As to Samantha Brad beer, filer, and antiquarian for Trademark Cards, Inc., early valentines-creators drove the manufacture and unfold of gambling playing cards in England and the USA — Jonathan Lord of London and Esther Howland of Worcester, Massachusetts. "Lord led surprising ribbon paper and superb method the usage of bits of glitter, feathers, and blooms as decorations.

Howland, stirred with the aid of manner of English ribbon valentines, started manufacturing ornate valentines which supplied for as an entire lot as $50 apiece at some degree inside the 1850s," makes experience of Brad beer.

By the mid-19th hundred years, every England and the us had big scope valentine introduction frameworks set up. Offending valentines advanced conventional valentines and supplied producers with a similarly wellspring of coins.

Vinegar gambling cards might be inexpensively created through printing them on a single piece of paper, collapsing, and fixing them with a touch of wax. All subjects considered; Brad beer affords that many economically made gambling playing cards of the 19th century had remarkable guide work of their gathering.

While the U.S. Dependancy of changing valentines did no longer increase until after the Nationwide War, across the lake valentine fever started out aggressively about the equal period because the postal shift.

England's Uniform Penny Post, which permit everyone in Britain mail some component thru the located up place of work for sincerely one penny, have turn out to be real on January 10, 1840.

After one year, the public sent almost a half of million valentines. In 1871, London's postal station processed 1.2 million playing playing cards. The variety may additionally additionally have been bigger, despite the fact that postmasters now after which grabbed vinegar valentines, believing them overly profane for delivery.

Mailmen had been not through the use of any way the most effective ones disturbed with the resource in their terribleness of vinegar cards. "There are cutting-edge documents from diaries and papers that display that clench fist fight and criminal arguments, self-destruction and attempted homicide happened," writes Dust.

The Pall Shopping Center Paper of London issued a piece of writing about his estranged in 1885 approximately a companion's partner after she delivered him a vinegar valentine.

Not many Vinegar Valentines Cards Were Protected

Less is had a few massive information of disturbing valentines than nostalgic ones, to a restrained degree in slight of the reality that now not very many made due. "There are private documents that reveal recipients burned them and gobbled them from humiliation.

Most lasting models are unsent playing cards tracked down in the assortments of printers and stationers," Dust makes feel of.

Since they have been mailed covertly, most exporters of vinegar valentines encountered now not many outcomes. Compounding an already hard situation, shippers didn't simply foot the rate of postage.

"Not inside the least did vinegar valentines have quite slanderous justifications; but, they have been moreover conveyed cash on delivery (cash down) and rate the recipient one cent to test," states Brad beer.

Because of a part of the extreme comments and common letters of criticism inside the news, the gambling cards commenced out to end up unwanted. " Some condemned the card manufacturers for crass profits-chasing, whilst others accused the tendencies of the freshly informed population who can also need to attend to the price of those tiny items.

Whether trade or class have turn out to be the reason for their increase, competitive desires to smooth up the holiday came out to be more countless inside the later-19th 100 years, Dust states.

Today, on occasion many Valentine's Day playing cards painting this form of horrible spirit. Yet, Dust thinks a contemporary-day equivalent for savage and unknown parallels exists: the internet-based entertainment savage.

Who Was the Genuine St. Valentine?

The Numerous Fantasies Behind the Motivation for Valentine's Day

There had been numerous St. Valentines (which encompass beheaded ones), nonetheless, it emerge as a middle age creator who firstly steady the vacation's passionate manner of lifestyles.

On February 14, whilst we change chocolates, tremendous dinners, or doily playing cards with our pals and own family, we do it for the purpose of Holy Saint Valentine. Yet, who was this holy individual of sentiment?

Search the internet, and you could track down masses of anecdotes about him — or them. One Holy person Valentine have become sincerely a Roman clergyman who completed covert marriages no matter the options of the specialists inside the 1/3 100 years.

Detained on the house of an honorable, he recuperated his detainer's sight-handicapped daughter, making the complete circle of relatives transformed to Christianity and putting his destiny. Prior to being tortured and decapitated on February 14, he gave the younger girl a message inscribed "Your Valentine."

A few reviews endorse every different saintly character called Valentine all through a comparable technology come to be the Diocesan of Terni, additionally related with mystery marriages and struggling by using way of execution on February 14.

Tragically for the ones looking forward to a clean, passionate records to the event, lecturers who've studied its origins trust there can be a minimum motive for the ones data. As a rely of reality, Valentine's Day actually were given associated with love inside the past due Medieval periods, due to the English writer Geoffrey Chaucer.

"The times that everybody cites, the diocese and the cleric, they're just like the factor where it makes me dubious," says Bruce Forbes, a professor of hard checks at Morningside School in Iowa.

Different Martyred Holy Person Valentines

Valentine turn out to be a alternatively recognized call in historical Rome, and there aren't any fewer than 50 memories of various holy individuals of that name. However, Forbes said the oldest extant payments of the 2 February 14 Valentines, recorded beginning about the 500s, percent a ton for all functions and capabilities. Both were believed to have repaired a little one at the same time as jailed, causing a own family-massive stringent alternate, and that they were completed throughout the equal time of the 12 months and covered along a similar thruway.

The actual proof is tough to the diploma wherein it is not enjoyable if the narrative originated with one holy character who subsequently have grow to be or on the other hand whether biographers of one guy received subtleties from the other — or as an alternative if both at any factor existed altogether.

Maybe more hard for the emotional human beings among us, the early money owed of the two Valentines are traditional suffering recollections, targeted at the holy humans's miracles and ghastly passing on the equal time as which encompass nary a word about feeling.

"They're every well-known besides, and the reference to loving is extensively extra legendary," says Henry Kelly, a expert of middle age and renaissance literature and information at UCLA.

Following Valentine's Day to Lupercalia

Holy man or woman, Valentine's Day has additionally been related with a Christian try to replace the greater established competition of Lupercalia, which Romans determined on February 15. A few present-day legends portray Lupercalia as a completely scorching party, at the same time as ladies wrote their names on dust pills which men in the end drew from a area, bringing together abnormal pairings.

Once all over again, be that as it could, early documents don't guide this. The closest covered up among Lupercalia and contemporary-day Valentine's Day traditions is via all debts that the Roman competition worried certainly nude young lads placing every person spherical them with shreds of goat pores and skin.

As consistent with the historical writer Plutarch, a few younger married ladies referred to that obtaining struck with the skins better origination and simple artwork.

Anything tiny emotive sentiments also can had been important for Lupercalia; they did now not represent the brand new Christian birthday party.

"It in reality makes me nuts that the Roman fantasy is forever flowing," Forbes provides. "The reality for me is until Chaucer we haven't any evidence of all people appearing something in particular superb and sincere on February 14."

Chapter 9: 6 Astounding Realities About St. Valentine

Who become St. Valentine, and for what motive are we able to honor him on February 14? Get up to date realities approximately this enigmatic individual.

1. St. Valentine who enlivened the occasion could have been fantastic humans.

Officially appeared by means of the usage of the Roman Catholic Church, St. Valentine is taken into consideration to be a actual decide who exceeded on to the amazing past about A.D. 270. Notwithstanding, his real individuality changed into addressed as speedy as A.D. 496 through way of Pope Gelasius I, who referred to the saint and his travels approximately as "being mentioned best to God.

" One chronicle from the 1400s suggests Valentine as a sanctuary priest who turned into beheaded close to Rome with the aid of using the sovereign Claudius II for assisting Christian couples with weddings unique account indicates Valentine emerge as the Cleric of Terni, also martyred through Claudius II at the borders of Rome.

Due to the likenesses of those files, it is suggested they may hint at a comparable person. Enough uncertainty covers the real character of St. Valentine that the Catholic Church halted formal adoration of him in 1969, no matter the truth that his call remains on its rundown of formally appeared holy parents.

2. On the whole, there are kind of twelve St. Valentines, in addition to a pope.

The saintly determine we commemorate on Valentine's Day is recognized formally as St. Valentine of Rome to distinguish him from the dozen or so exceptional Valentines on the list. Since "Valentinus" — from the Latin phrase which means, big regions of energy for noteworthy strong — turned into a well known moniker a number of the second one and 8th hundred years A.D., some saints in some unspecified time in the future of the course of the loads of years have imparted this appellation.

The reliable Roman Catholic utility of saintly human beings indicates greater or a great deal less twelve who've been known as Valentines or a few version thereof. The maximum of late exalted Valentine is St. Valentine Berrio-Ochoa, a Spaniard of the Dominican order who undertook a voyage to Vietnam, wherein he crammed in as diocese until his execution in 1861. Pope John Paul II consecrated Barrio-Ochoa in 1988.

There modified into additionally a Pope Valentine, irrespective of the fact that now not anything is thought about him with the exception that he served a brief forty days spherical A.D. 827.

three. Valentine is the benefactor holy man or woman of beekeepers and epilepsy, amongst endless tremendous topics.

Holy people are definitely predicted to stay lively inside the afterlife. Their wonderful duties embody intervening in herbal efforts and tasty appeals from residing spirits. In this manner, St. Valentine has very large duties. Individuals approach him to have a look at after the lifestyles of darlings, clearly, but in addition to mediation on the subject of beekeeping and epilepsy, in addition to the plague, blacking out, and voyaging.

As you can expect, he is also the supporter holy individual of associated couples and high-quality partnerships.

four. You can trace down Valentine's cranium in Rome.

The blossom-adorned skull of St. Valentine is in simple view on the Basilica of St Nick Maria in Cosmedin, Rome.

In the mid-1800s, the unearthing of a tomb near Rome exposed skeleton remnant quantities and distinct artifacts in recent times diagnosed with St. Valentine. As is ordinary, those fragments and bits of the overdue holy character's corpse have correspondingly been assigned to reliquaries all around the earth. You'll are trying to find down various bits of St. Valentine's skeleton in simple view during the Czech Republic, Ireland, Scotland, Britain, and France.

5. English artist Geoffrey Chaucer need to have invented Valentine's Day.

The middle age English artist Geoffrey Chaucer often misused statistics, casting his lovely figures inner imagined verifiable occasions that he addressed as real. No hint exists of emotional activities on Valentine's Day preceding to a poem Chaucer authored approximately 1375. In his work "Parliament of Foules," he ties a exercise of adorable love with the opposition of St. Valentine's dining revel in day-an attachment that did not exist until after his sonnet garnered unavoidable scrutiny.

The sonnet pertains to February 14 because of the truth the day birds (and people) meet collectively to are looking for and discover a mate. The thing wherein Chaucer remarked,

"For this have become dispatched on Saint Valentine's Day/When every foul cometh there to pick out out his mate," he can also want to have invented the competition we apprehend in recent times.

6. You may additionally have a good time Valentine's Day some times every year.

In slight of the overflow of St. Valentines at the Roman Catholic listing, you would possibly pick out to laud the holy person on severa days each twelve months. Other than February 14, you may choose to honor St. Valentine of Viterbo on November 3. Or as an alternative, maybe you want to get a jump on the typical Valentine's competition thru feting St.

Valentine of Raetia on January 7. Ladies would likely pick out to worship the most girl St. Valentine (Valentina), a virgin slain in Palestine on July 25, A.D. 308. The Eastern Conventional Church formally honors St. Valentine instances, as quickly as as a senior of the congregation on July 6 and as quickly as as a saint on July 30.

Valentine's Day Realities

Find out about St. Valentine's Day's actual significance, its origins, and beginnings, how it's far applauded, why we are announcing "naked the entirety to all bystanders," and considerably extra.

Valentine's Day is hailed on February 14 when couples over the area commemorate their buddies, accomplices, and darlings. Many prolonged lengths of traditions and customs have brought on it into the vacation that we be aware nowadays. The following are nine thrilling truths approximately the holiday devoted to feeling and love.

Beginnings of a Ridiculous Agnostic Celebration

Some connect Valentine's Day origins to a Christian try to supersede an agnostic ripening opposition that has been dated as decrease back because the 6th century B.C.

During the celebration of Lupercalia, Roman clerics may forfeit goats and dogs and make use of their blood-sopping moist stows away to slap ladies in the town, as a ripeness favoring.

As in keeping with folklore, women may also in the long run deposit their names in an urn and be picked to be partnered with a person for a 12 months.

Letters Addressed to 'Juliet'

Consistently, a wonderful many sensitive people write letters addressed to Verona, Italy to "Juliet," the challenge of the well-known heartbreaking disaster, "Romeo and Juliet." The town represents the place of the Shakespearean tale, and the letters that come to the metropolis are dutifully spoke back to via the usage of the use of a set of personnel from the Juliet Club.

Every three hundred and sixty five days, on Valentine's Day, the club offers the "Cara Giulietta" ("Dear Juliet") trophy to the originator of the maximum absurdly romantic love letter.

Box of Chocolates

The Valentine's Day addiction of delivering a discipline of sweets became based totally inside the nineteenth one hundred years with the beneficial aid of Richard Cadbury, a descendant of an English chocolate assembling dynasty. With a few other method as of late decided at the corporation to fabricate greater assortments of chocolate, Cadbury leaped at the feasible opportunity to marketplace the sweets as a factor of the cherished event.

First Valentine Was Composed of a Jail

History's maximum iconic valentine modified into penned in probable one of the most unromantic settings feasible: a jail. Charles, Duke of Orleans penned the loving letter to his 2d marriage at 21 years antique at the same time as captured at the Clash of Agincourt. As a captive for over decades, he should in no manner get maintain of his valentine's solution to the sonnet he wrote to her in the mid-fifteenth one hundred years.

'Vinegar Valentines' Beat Admirers down

During the Victoria Period, the those who did no longer require the regard of specific fanatics may also want to surreptitiously supply "vinegar valentines." These cards, regularly dubbed penny dreadful, were the intense antithesis of everyday valentines, hilariously traumatic and rejecting undesired suitors. They had been then employed to intention suffragettes within the late 19th and mid-twentieth hundred years.

'Bearing the whole lot to all bystanders'

The statement "exposing coronary heart and soul to all observers" also can have starting factors in deciding on a valentine. Smithsonian states that at some diploma within the Medieval Ages, guys may want to pick the names of ladies that they may be coupled with for the upcoming year at the same time as attending a Roman rite approximately Juno. Subsequent after choice, the person adult males wore the names on their sleeves to show their dating at some point of the merriments.

'Darlings' Confections Began as Tablets

The superb light coronary heart-molded confections that have been dished out fondly every Valentine's Day originated as capsules. As indicated with the resource of the usage of the Food Business News, medication expert, and innovator Oliver Pursue built a tool that could immediately produce the medication previous to converting to using the tool to make candies – in a while called Necco Wafers.

Pursuer's brother conceived of the notion to print phrases at the candy in 1866, and the confections obtained their coronary coronary heart shape in 1901, attractive mainly to Valentine's Day darlings.

Cupid Started as a Greek God

The tubby teenager with wings and a bow and bolt that we name Cupid has been associated with Valentine's Day for pretty a long time. Notwithstanding, earlier than he modified into nicknamed Cupid, he turn out to be recounted to the historical Greeks as Eros, the keep near of adoration. Eros, the child of the Greek goddess Aphrodite, need to use arrangements of bolts — one for adoration and one extra for despise — to toy with the emotions of his desires. It changed into best after evaluations of his underhandedness were relayed via way of Romans that he regular the harmless element that we have a look at now.

How 'X' Came to Actually Mean 'Kiss'

Utilizing a kiss to approve valentines likewise has a lengthy statistics, as indicated with the aid of the use of way of the Washington Post. The use of "X" began to deal with Christianity, or the circulate, inside the Medieval intervals. During a comparable event, the image turn out to be hired to approve facts. Subsequent to confirming with an X, the author would generally kiss the affect as a photo in their vow.

As the signal advanced among lords and commonplace humans to protect books, letters, and desk tough art work, the ones facts had been described as having been "steady with a kiss."

How Chocolate Turned right right into a Valentine's Day Staple

Is it in moderate of chocolate's purported sexual enhancer functions, or merely a way for sweet groups to promote extra chocolates within the hole amongst Christmas and Easter?

Discussion hearts, truffles abounding, and heart-molded packing containers of goodies — those are the imagery of Valentine's Day for wonderful sweethearts all sooner or later of the earth. However, wherein did this life-style upward thrust up from? While the middle underpinnings of Valentine's Day achieve as some distance as feasible lower back to Roman instances, actual present-giving is a far overdue turn of affairs.

Valentine's Day is surely named after separate Roman holy human beings, every called Valentine and each totally unattached to emotional love. However, the story survives that the genuine St. Valentine modified right into a preacher who accomplished illicit connections for Ruler Claudius' officials, however there may be no proof to imply this often befell.

The important be aware about St. Valentine's Day as an emotional competition came up inside the works of Geoffrey Chaucer in 1382. With the middle age term got here extra focus on illicit however natural dignified love, and it's miles right here that we see a chunk of the natural iconographies begin to reveal up. Knights would possibly deliver flora to their better halves and extol their greatness in songs from a remote location.

In any event, sugar become as but a precious substance in Europe, for this reason there was no concept of swapping or affords.

To apprehend greater about History of Chocolate, search for one in every of my books on Amazon

Titled: CHOCOLATE: The Untold History of Chocolate

Who Made the Primary Valentine's Day Box of Chocolates?

By the 1840s, the belief of Valentine's Day as a festival to commemorate genuine love had taken over the larger part of the English-talking globe.

It modified into Cupid's brilliant age: The pedantic Victorians loved the idea of amazing love and showered each exceptional with hard gambling playing cards and offers. Into this passionate heated combat stepped Richard Cadbury, scion of an English chocolate assembling dynasty and answerable for negotiations at an urgent time in his company's facts.

Cadbury had as of overdue greater appropriate their chocolate-manufacturing tool a extraordinary way to disentangle unadulterated cocoa margarine from whole beans, making more adorable eating chocolate than most Britons had at any factor tasted.

This cycle added in a further diploma of cocoa margarine, which Cadbury applied to generate a number of assortments of what come to be then dubbed "consuming chocolate." Richard discovered an first-rate showcasing threat for the glowing sweets and commenced out presenting them in beautifully adorned containers that he genuinely created.

Starting there, it changed into a quick bounce to take the acquainted images of Cupids and vegetation and location them on coronary heart-normal bins. While Richard Cadbury did no longer simply patent the coronary

coronary heart-usual field, it is normally believed that he became rapid to make one.

Cadbury marketed the instances as having a twofold reason: When the sweets had all been ate up, the actual crate changed into attractive to the element that it very well may be employed time and over to save treasures, from strands of hair to recognize letters.

The cases were extra elaborate until the flare-up of The Second Great War even as sugar modified into confined and Valentine's Day celebrations were shriveled. Yet, Victorian-time Cadbury containers do exist, and many are precious family legacies or essential artifacts prized through gatherers.

Chapter 10: History's Most Hooked Up Realized Valentine Was Written In Jail

A French center age duke authored the sonnet to his better love whilst he changed into taken captive within the Pinnacle of London.

Valentine's Day is the handiest competition supposed for demonstrating devotion and warmth.

Be that as it can, the statistics inside the returned of the most seasoned located out valentine entails a tale of royal in-preventing, war, and detainment in a center age tower.

The "valentine" itself modified into essentially a couple of strains in a sonnet, authored with the aid of way of the usage of Charles, the Duke of Orléans, in 1415,

whilst he turn out to be 21 years of age. Charles spent his upbringing in a peevish French well-known own family.

As the nephew of Lord Charles VI of France, otherwise referred to as Charles the

Distraught (who have grow to be famous to be schizophrenic), he emerge as trapped within the crossfire between his dad, Louis I, who managed the Place of Orléans, and his uncle's own family, which supervised the Place of Burgundy, of their warfare for manipulate of France.

Like different royals of the duration, Charles' married lifestyles concerned reputation, no longer a coronary heart.

At age 12, he modified into given to his 17-three hundred and sixty five days-vintage cousin and small daughter of Lord Charles VI, Isabella of Valois, currently a widow inside the aftermath of having first of all hitched at age six.

After a one year, catastrophe struck at the same time as Charles' dad Louis I, have come to be slain, and his mum hit the bucket quickly lengthy. Charles and his brothers pledged revenge on their maximum remembered relative John the Brave, the Duke of Burgundy, whom they accused of murdering their dad in a energy take keep of, deepening the circle of relatives countrywide conflict.

Charles' more youthful courting with Isabella ceased speedy after it began while she surpassed on to the high-quality beyond generating an offspring in 1409. The following three hundred and sixty 5 days, Charles changed into wedded in a unmarried greater political partnership — this event to eleven-3 hundred and sixty 5 days-vintage Bonne of Armagnac, daughter of Bernard VII, Count of Armagnac, and capability Constable of France.

Their marriage set up the relationship many of the two lineages.

It furthermore positioned the adolescent duke in his father thru marriage's Armagnac camp in the years-lengthy French national conflict among the Armagnacs and the Burgundians.

As severa conflicts have been not on time a number of the opposing factions, Charles was captured and held through the Burgundians in 1415. While positioned beneath lockdown in the Pinnacle of London, he penned a sonnet to his massive one of a kind the proper year that he have become captured at the Clash of Agincourt.

In the sonnet, Charles employs the phrase "Valentine" concerning his large one in all a kind, despite the fact that his appearance of adores emerge as graver than the holiday appropriate tidings that we are typically familiar with.

In any occasion, considering the lousy conditions beneath which the letter have become penned, this is not something surprising.

My notably super Valentine,

Since for me, you've got been conceived too early,

Also, I for you turned into conceived beyond the aspect of no move lower back.

God excuses him who has estranged

Me from you for the entire 365 days.

I'm as of now bored of admiration,

My in particular sensitive Valentine.

Having been held for pretty a long time, Charles become constantly now not able to view his better half of of's answer successfully. She surpassed away in some unspecified time inside the future someplace in the region of 1430 and 1435, earlier than reconnecting in conjunction with her outstanding one-of-a-kind or having any babies.

Past the Valentine he mailed off Isabella, Charles produced severa other sonnets while in prison — many concerning devotion and honorability. Be that as it is able to, the longer he end up in confinement, the hazier his poetry had been given. His work is now to be had and tailor-made into English in some courses, substantially "The Sonnets of Charles Orleans," via the use of Sally Purcell.

Years after Bonne's passing, Charles traveled another time to France and changed into wedded, at age 46, to Mary of Cleves, 14. They proceeded to have three babies. He perished away in 1465.

7 Groundbreaking Kisses in History

From Judas to 15 August 1945 to an interracial Star Trip adventure, discover what kisses made a few fundamental impact ever.

Notwithstanding what the melody says, a kiss isn't generally most effective a kiss. A kiss can be political, whether or not or now not or no longer as it's the primary of its kind or in slight of the reality that it's among heads of country. A kiss can likewise grow to be superb even as it is stuck on film, irrespective of whether or not or no longer the actual kiss modified into intrusive or unwanted.

In light of that, here's a rundown of possibly the maximum paramount kisses ever.

1. First Recorded Kiss (spherical 1500 B.C.) (spherical 1500 B.C.)

Researchers banter approximately whether kissing started out as a pattern that unfold all around the planet, or jumped up obviously in numerous locales. Regardless, the earliest mentioned composed notices of it are in Vedic Sanskrit sacred texts round 1500 B.C., as consistent with research with the useful resource of Vaughn Bryant, a human research professor at Texas A&M College. These sacred writings, known as the Vedas, have been relevant to the religion of Hinduism.

From that factor ahead, kissing stored on showing up in antique Indian and Hindu writing. The Mahabharata, a Sanskrit epic ordered via the fourth century A.D., has a line in which any person "set her mouth to my mouth and made a commotion that created delight in me." The Kamasutra likewise has a element on kissing that acknowledges diverse techniques for kissing and varieties of kisses.

2. Judas' Kiss (circa first Century A.D.) (round first Century A.D.)

Kissing isn't best a sincere display. It additionally may be a hallmark of fellowship or disloyalty. In the Stories of the great statistics of Matthew and Imprint, written about the primary one hundred years, Judas deceives Jesus with the useful resource of manner of distinguishing him with a kiss so that armed guys could probably do away with him and, in the end, run murder him.

Judas' kiss has in the end turn out to be a well-known narrative reference. It must have enlivened the "kiss of dying" that comes up in mafia fiction and movies (despite the fact that changed into possibly never a real mafia exercising) (but end up probably in no way a actual mafia workout). Maybe the most famous example is in The Backup determine Part II at the same time as Al Pacino's ego offers his brother Fredo the kiss of loss of life for promoting out him.

3. First Kiss on Film (1896) (1896)

The primary humans to kiss in video shape had been May Irwin and John C. Rice, who confirmed up in a quick movie referred to variably as May Irwin kiss, Kiss, or The Kiss. In 1896, the two performers traveled to Thomas Edison's studio in New Jersey and reenacted their very last kiss scene from a play they had been performing in New York City.

In the the the front of an target marketplace, no one felt the kiss turn out to be most effective unexpected. Be that as it could, numerous fondled the surrounding images of them kissing became too wicked.

4. First Dark Kiss on Film (1898) (1898)

In 1898, dark entertainers' Holy man or woman Suttle and Gertie Brown participated in a quick movie entitled Something Great Negro Kiss, the primary film to painting darkish Americans kissing.

In 2017, movie college students of data unearthed the tape, which became filmed thru manner of a white man known as William Selig in Chicago.

"There's an exhibition there thinking about they'll be hitting the dance floor with every different, but, their kissing has an plain feeling of effortlessness, pleasure, and leisure too," Allyson Nadia Field, a professor of film and media learns at the College of Chicago who diagnosed the film, said in a university public declaration. "It is extraordinarily excellent to me, as a data researcher who works with race and cinema, to conceive that this form of curio may moreover moreover have existed in 1898."

5. 15 august 1945 Kiss (1945) (1945)

On the morning of August 14, 1945, sufferers came into Greta Zimmer's Manhattan administrative center promising the combat in Japan have grow to be finished. The Austrian migrant did now not sure what to think, so on her mid-day harm, she walked to Times Square in her white dentist colleague's costume to check what the facts ticker said. The temper there has been satisfied, and the ticker bolstered that it grow to be in truth V-J

Day, and The Second Great War changed into executed.

As Zimmer became faraway from the ticker, a Naval stress mariner named George Mendonsa — who'd started out out eating early and incorrect Zimmer for a scientific attendant — came up and violently kissed her, leaving his lover.

Zimmer tried to push the outdoor off, and they prompt in opposite methods. In any occasion, unknown to the two of them, image shooters Alfred Eisenstaedt and Victor Jorgensen had each captured the immediately, as documented in The Kissing Mariner: The Secret Behind the Photograph that Finished the Second Great War.

Eisenstaedt's shot became one of the most well-known WWII pics in U.S. History, to some detail because spectators mistook it for an photo of a Maritime officer and medical attendant getting collectively to have an high-quality time.

The picture has likewise mingled debate, as severa people have assured over the route of the years to be the pair within the picture, on the same time as a few deliver up that it suggests a nonconsensual second.

Zimmer, herself, placed in a meeting with the Library of Congress in 2005, "It wasn't my preference to be kissed...The gentleman honestly came up and kissed or grabbed!"

6. Star Trip Interracial Kiss (1968) (1968)

At the time even as William Shatner and Nichelle Nichols kissed in a 1968 episode of Star Trip, it grow to be no longer, in reality, the number one interracial kiss on U.S. TV. Yet, it turn out to be the fine that seemed to have the biggest societal have an impact on.

In the episode, called "Plato's Stepchildren," Chief James Kirk and Officer Nyota Uhura come upon intruders who pressure them to kiss every other via magical strength.

In Nichols' ebook Past Uhura: Star Trip and Different Recollections, she recounts that NBC modified into involved about the way wherein white Americans must react to the immediate, in order that they ordered that the performers shoot scenes: one with a kiss and one with out a kiss. In any occasion, Nichols and Shatner purposefully botched up each one of the kisses a lot much less takes to make sure that NBC confirmed the kissing series.

7. Communist Intimate Kiss (1979) (1979)

During the Virus War, rulers of socialist regimes regularly greeted an additional with what's referred to as the "communist intimate kiss." This might be at the cheek or the lips, even though the maximum prominent model is French photographs artist Régis Bosso's 1979 shot of the Soviet Association's Leonid Brezhnev and East Germany's Erich Honecker kissing at the mouth.

The kiss passed off whilst Brezhnev visited East Berlin to laud the 30th remembrance of the German Popularity-primarily based

Republic (i.E., East Germany) (i.E., East Germany).

At the time while the Berlin Wall have end up down in 1989, the Soviet artisan Dmitri Vrubel replicated the picture in a painting on the wall's east aspect.

He entitled it: "My God, Assist Me in Enduring This Dangerous Love."

Chapter 11: 10 Things You Didn't Know Occurred On Valentine's Day

Valentine's Day is loaded with playing cards, flowers, and goodies however pretty some history too.

1. Commander James Cook is killed: 1779

Among England's most a achievement pioneers, Cook diagrammed regions from Newfoundland to New Zealand to Gold united states of the us. In 1778, on his 1/3 tour to the Pacific Sea, he changed and feature come to be the primary European on report to visit the Hawaiian Islands and changed into welcomed with honor.

He experienced a pretty unique collecting, however, while he returned the subsequent 12 months.

After one of the commercial enterprise organisation's tiny boats become abducted, the captain opted to fight decrease again, no longer with the aid of the use of setting onto his very personal boat, however as an opportunity via retaining Hawaiian Ruler Kalaniopuu locked down all else being equal. A hostile crowd enveloped Cook and his soldiers once they landed at Kealakekua Straight with the ruler.

At the time that phrase came up that the outsiders had shot a neighboring tribe leader across the sound, the gang headed after. Cook shot little time useless though in advance than he must reload, the captain changed into pounded on the pinnacle and slashed time and again previous to kicking the bucket in the knee-profound seas.

2. Skirmish of Pot River: 1779

As Cook combat the unfriendly horde in Hawaii, his colleagues were embroiled in a single extra warfare large extensive sort of miles distant. In likely of the heaviest combat in Georgia within the route of the American Unrest, 4 hundred nationalists fired out an sudden attack on a band of approximately 800 Followers from North and South Carolina that had set up camp along the beaten Pot River inside the woodlands of Wilkes District.

Despite the fact that dwarfed, the nationalist nation navy earned a definitive achievement and aided with subduing the English approaches to detach the southern settlements from those within the mid-Atlantic and New Britain.

three. Oregon turns into a kingdom: 1859

With the stroke of President James Buchanan's pen, Oregon grow to be common because the 33rd state within the Association actually years earlier than it might be decimated via way of the Nationwide war. Oregon had burned through 11 years as a US region, and it'd need almost a month for trendy statistics about its front to traverse the dominion from Washington, D.C. Via a combination of radio, stagecoach, and steamer.

4. Alexander Graham Ringer files for mobile phone patent: 1876

In the extended length of America's centennial, a criminal counselor addressing Chime recorded his cellphone patent utility on the U.S. Patent Office in Washington, D.C., simplest hours earlier than the legal professional for Elisha Dark documented a proviso reporting his reason to document a case for a patent for his rendition of a smartphone.

Given the two petitions, the Patent Office in the long run resolved on Walk 7, 1876, to trouble the most critical patent for a telephone, US Patent No. 174,465, to Chime.

After 3 days in Boston, Chime skillfully communicated communique through smartphone cables even as he addressed those terms to his associate, "Mr. Watson — Come right here — I need to appearance you." The jail combat amongst Ringer and Dark carried on for a fairly extended duration.

5. General William Tecumseh Sherman dies on 1891

Inside his house at the Upper West Side of New York City, the aged champion bowed to infection and died at 71 years antique. President Benjamin Harrison, who had served beneath the overall within the Nationwide war, asked all public banners to be flown at half of-pole to understand the Association favored who's merciless 1864 "Walk to the Ocean" ended in a warfare location at some stage in Georgia and ended up being one of the warfare's definitive minutes.

Three preceding presidents and each one of the commanders who had served under him went to Sherman's memorial ceremony in advance than his corpse, carrying a entire army uniform, end up transported to St. Louis for interment.

6. Arizona turns into a kingdom: 1912

In greater of fifty years after Oregon joined the Association on Valentine's Day, Arizona did likewise. President William Howard Taft at the start rejected Arizona's petition for statehood in 1911 in moderate of the reality that its charter authorized courtroom docket have a look at. After Arizona bad the problematic provision, Taft made the statement to mention it the 48th state.

Arizona electors parted appreciably on Final voting day in 1912, regardless of the fact that, after they authorised a blanketed revision reinstating judicial assessment and gave Taft only thirteen% of their votes, setting him within the lower back of Woodrow Wilson, Theodore Roosevelt, and Eugene V. Debs.

7. Jimmy Hoffa is conceived: in 1913

While the employee's guild leader's decisive fate remained unknown, there may be no thriller defensive the start of his lifestyles.

Hoffa turn out to be introduced into the sector on Valentine's Day in Brazil, Indiana. Subsequent to advancing via the affiliation posts to end up head of the Teamsters 1957 and serving time in prison in jail for a payoff, Hoffa disappeared from the car parking space of a Detroit restaurant on July

31, 1975, and has in no manner been seen due to the fact.

eight. The besieging of Dresden: 1945

In the very last, a completely lengthy period of The Second Great War, English, and American plane made an overpowering flying assault on the well-known capital of the japanese German province of Saxony.

The firestorm that ignited from the preliminary spherical of excessive-volatile bombs and combustible devices that have been dropped truely minutes after 12 PM have become tremendous to this sort of degree that aircraft pilots inside the following wave have to see the sparkle from 500 miles away.

The large -day air attack demolished ninety% of the downtown area, wrecked social fortunes, and murdered somewhere within the form of 35,000 and 130 five,000, a endless gauge because it changed into mysterious the sizeable form of refugees that had been inside the city at that factor. The besieging modified into complex due to the fact Dresden modified into neither essential to German wartime advent nor a number one modern metropolis.

nine. First Knesset assembly: 1949

Months inside the following obtaining independence, Israel's maximum awesome parliament, the Constituent Get collectively, convened interior short quarters in Jerusalem's Jewish Organization constructing. Israel's most remembered president, Chaim Weizmann, imparted a excessive region in which he provided "kinship to all concord cherishing humans" and advanced a "hand of harmony" to the usa of a's Bedouin buddies earlier to swearing inside the 100 twenty parliamentarians. After days, the parliament dubbed itself the Knesset. It relocated into its relatively long lasting housing in Jerusalem in 1966.

10. Jacqueline Kennedy flaunts the White House: 1962.

Wearing a triple strand of pearls and a pink fleece get dressed suiting Valentine's Day, the 32-one year-antique First Woman drove a gargantuan waft-country TV intention market tuned into CBS and NBC on a virtual journey throughout the White House's united states of the united states rooms, which she had as of late repaired.

Joined thru manner of CBS newsman Charles Collingwood, Mrs. Kennedy exhibited her expertise of expressive arts as she furnished the first rate house's great representations, collections, and devices.

Despite the truth that President John F. Kennedy arrived there for the very last five minutes of the broadcast, his higher 1/2 of have become the movie well-known man or woman, obtaining vital acclamations and a distinguished Emmy Award.

Chapter 12: Account Of Saint Valentine

Numerous early Christian martyrs have been named Valentine. The Valentines venerated on February 14 are Valentine of Rome (Valentines press. M. Rome) and Valentine of Terni (Valentines ep. Interamnensis m. Romae). Valentine of Rome has come to be a clergyman in Rome who became martyred in 269. He turned into brought to the calendar of saints with the aid of Pope Gelasius I in 496 and end up buried at the Via Flaminia. The relics of Saint Valentine have been saved in the Church and Catacombs of San Valentino in Rome, which "remained an vital pilgrim website on-line at some point of the Middle Ages until the relics of St. Valentine were transferred to the church of Santa Prassede at a few level within the hold forth of Nicholas IV".] The flower-crowned cranium of Saint Valentine is exhibited inside the Basilica of Santa Maria in Cosmedin, Rome. Other relics are located at Whitefriar Street Carmelite Church in Dublin, Ireland.

Valentine of Terni have come to be bishop of Interamna, now Terni, in critical Italy, and is stated to were martyred during the persecution beneath Emperor Aurelian in 273. He is buried on the Via Flaminia, but in a special area from Valentine of Rome. His relics are at the Basilica of Saint Valentine in Terni (Basilica di San Valentino). Professor Jack B. Oruch of the University of Kansas notes that "abstracts of the acts of the 2 saints were in nearly each church and monastery of Europe."The Catholic Encyclopedia speaks of a third saint named Valentine who emerge as stated in early martyrologies underneath date of February 14. He changed into martyred in Africa with some of partners, but now not anything extra is notion about him. A relic claimed to be Saint Valentine of Terni's head changed into preserved within the abbey of New Minster, Winchester, and venerated.

February 14 is celebrated as St. Valentine's Day in numerous Christian denominations; it has, for instance, the rank of 'commemoration' in the calendar of saints inside the Anglican Communion.The dinner party day of Saint Valentine is given in the calendar of saints of the Lutheran Church. However, in the 1969 revision of the Roman Catholic Calendar of Saints, the night meal day of Saint Valentine on February 14 changed into removed from the General Roman Calendar and relegated to unique (neighborhood or even national) calendars for the following cause: "Though the memorial of Saint Valentine is antique,it's far left to specific calendars, because of the fact, aside from his call, not anything is concept of Saint Valentine besides that he modified into buried at the Via Flaminia on February 14.

The ceremonial dinner day is widely known in Balzan (Malta) where relics of the saint are claimed to be positioned, and additionally within the direction of the arena thru Traditionalist Catholics who test the older, pre-Second Vatican Council calendar (see General Roman Calendar of 1960).

Legends

J.C. Cooper, in The Dictionary of Christianity, writes that Saint Valentine changed into "a clergyman of Rome who turn out to be imprisoned for succouring persecuted Christians.Contemporary facts of Saint Valentine have been maximum in all likelihood destroyed in some unspecified time in the future of this Diocletianic Persecution within the early 4th century. In the 5th or sixth century, a chunk called Passio Marii et Marthae posted a tale of martyrdom for Saint Valentine of Rome, likely through borrowing tortures that befell to other saints, as modified into everyday within the literature of that length.

The equal activities are positioned in Bede's Martyrology, which turn out to be compiled in the eighth century.It states that Saint Valentine come to be persecuted as a Christian and interrogated via Roman Emperor Claudius II in man or woman. Claudius have grow to be inspired via

Valentine and had a speak with him, attempting to get him to convert to Roman paganism at the manner to maintain his existence. Valentine refused and attempted to convert Claudius to Christianity as an possibility. Because of this, he come to be finished. Before his execution, he is stated to have finished a miracle via way of recovery Julia, the blind daughter of his jailer Asterius. The jailer's daughter and his forty-six member family, family people and servants, got here to don't forget in Jesus and had been baptized.

A later Passio repeated the legend, including that Pope Julius I built a church over his sepulchre. (there is a confusion with a 4th-century tribune known as Valentino, who donated land to bring together a church at a time on the equal time as Julius have become a Pope).The legend changed into picked up as reality by means of the usage of later martyrologies, beginning with Bede's martyrology within the 8th century.It modified into repeated in the thirteenth century, in The Golden Legend.

There is a in addition embellishment to The Golden Legend, which steady with Henry Ansgar Kelly, have end up delivered in the 18th century and extensively repeated.On the night time time earlier than Valentine become to be completed, he is supposed to have written the primary "valentine" card himself, addressed to the daughter of his jailer Asterius, who have become no longer blind, signing as "Your Valentine".The expression "From your Valentine" become later observed with the aid of present day Valentine letters. This legend has been posted with the resource of each American Greetings and The History Channel.John Foxe, an English historian, in addition to the Order of Carmelites, united states of america that Saint Valentine became buried inside the Church of Praxedes in Rome, placed close to the cemetery of Saint Hippolytus. This order says that in step with legend, "Julia herself planted a pink-blossomed almond tree close to his grave. Today, the almond tree remains an brand of abiding love and friendship."

Another embellishment indicated that Saint Valentine finished clandestine Christian weddings for infantrymen who had been forbidden to marry. The Roman Emperor Claudius II supposedly forbade this so that you can boom his army, believing that married men did no longer make for proper infantrymen. However, George Monger writes that this marriage ban became by no means issued and that Claudius II instructed his infantrymen to take or three girls for themselves after his victory over the Goths.

According to legend, so as "to remind the ones men in their vows and God's love, Saint Valentine is said to have reduce hearts from parchment", giving them to those infantrymen and persecuted Christians, a probable foundation of the big use of hearts on St. Valentine's Day.

Saint Valentine supposedly wore a pink amethyst ring, normally worn on the hands of

Christian bishops with an photo of Cupid engraved in it, a recognizable image related to love that turn out to be criminal underneath the Roman Empire;] Roman soldiers could apprehend the ring and ask him to carry out marriage for them.Perhaps due to the affiliation with Saint Valentine, amethyst has become the birthstone of February, that is concept to draw love and affection.

Chapter 13: Folks Tradition

While the European folks traditions linked with Saint Valentine and St. Valentine's Day have become marginalized through cutting-edge-day customs connecting the day with romantic love, there are nevertheless a few connections with the arrival of spring.

While the custom of sending gambling playing playing cards, plant life, sweets and distinctive items emanated n the United Kingdom, Valentine's Day however remains associated with various neighborhood customs in England. In Norfolk, a person called 'Jack' Valentine knocks at the rear door of homes leaving sweets and parcels for kids. Although he turned into leaving treats, many kids have been fearful of this mystical character.

In Slovenia, Saint Valentine or Zdravko changed into one of the saints of spring, the saint of correct fitness and the consumer of beekeepers and pilgrims.] A proverb says that "Saint Valentine brings the keys of roots". Plants and flowers begin to develop on this day. It has been celebrated because the day while the number one art work in the vineyards and in the fields commences. It is likewise said that birds endorse to every high-quality or marry on that day. Another proverb says "Valentin – prvi spomladin" ("Valentine – the primary spring saint"), as in a few locations (particularly White Carniola), Saint Valentine marks the start of spring.

Valentine's Day has simplest these days been celebrated due to the fact the day of love. The day of love became historically March 12, the Saint Gregory's day, or February 22, Saint Vincent's Day. The consumer of love end up Saint Anthony, whose day has been celebrated on June thirteen.

St Valentine's Day's Connection with Romantic Love: Possible ancient origins

The "Feast" (Latin: "in natali", lit.: on the birthday) of Saint Valentine originated in Christendom and has been marked with the useful resource of the Western Church of Christendom in honour of one of the Christian martyrs named Valentine, as recorded in the eighth century Gelasian Sacramentary.In Ancient Rome, Lupercalia changed into discovered February 13–15 on behalf of Pan & Juno, pagan gods of love, marriage & fertility. It changed into a ceremony related to purification and health, and had most effective mild connection to fertility (as a part of health) and none to love. The birthday celebration of Saint Valentine is not recognized to have had any romantic connotations till Chaucer's poetry approximately "Valentine's Day" inside the 14th century, some seven-hundred years after party of Lupercalia is concept to have ceased.

Lupercalia grow to be a competition close by to the town of Rome. The greater well-known Festival of Juno Februa, because of this "Juno the cleaner" or "the chaste Juno", have end up celebrated on February thirteen–14. Although the Pope Gelasius I (492–496) article inside the Catholic Encyclopedia says that he abolished Lupercalia, theologian and

Methodist minister Bruce Forbes wrote that "no evidence" has been installed to hyperlink St. Valentine's Day and the rites of the ancient Roman purification festival of Lupercalia, regardless of claims thru many authors to the opposite.

Some researchers have theorized that Gelasius I changed Lupercalia with the party of the Purification of the Blessed Virgin Mary and claim a connection to the 14th century's connotations of romantic love, but there may be no historical indication that he ever meant this type of issue. Also, the dates do no longer in shape because of the fact at the time of Gelasius I, the dinner party become most effective celebrated in Jerusalem, and it turned into on February 14 most effective because Jerusalem positioned the Nativity of Jesus (Christmas) on January 6.[notes 3] Although it have become known as "Purification of the Blessed Virgin Mary", it furthermore handled the presentation of Jesus on the temple.Jerusalem's Purification of the Blessed Virgin Mary on February 14 have grow to be the Presentation of Jesus on the Temple on February 2 because it emerge as added to Rome and other places within the 6th century, after Gelasius I's time.

Alban Butler in his The Lives of the Fathers, Martyrs, and Other Principal Saints (1756–1759) claimed without proof that boys and ladies in Lupercalia drew names from a jar to make couples, and that cutting-edge Valentine's letters originated from this life-style. In fact, this practice originated within the Middle Ages, without a hyperlink to Lupercalia, with boys drawing the names of girls at random to couple with them. This custom was combated via monks, as an instance via Frances de Sales spherical 1600, apparently by means of the usage of manner of changing it with a religious custom of ladies drawing the names of apostles from the altar. However, this religious custom is recorded as quick due to the reality the thirteenth century within the life of Saint Elizabeth of Hungary, so it may have a first-rate basis.

The first recorded affiliation of Valentine's Day with romantic love is idea to be inside the Parliament of Fowls (1382) with the resource of Geoffrey Chaucer, a dream imaginative and prescient portraying a parliament for birds to select out their pals.Observing and honoring the primary anniversary of the engagement of fifteen-12 months-antique King Richard II of England to 15-12 months-vintage Anne of Bohemia, Chaucer wrote (in Middle English):

"For this changed into on seynt Valentynes day

Whan each foul cometh there to chese his make

Of every kynde that guys thynke may additionally

And that so huge a noyse gan they make

That erthe, and eyr, and tre, and every lake

So ful modified into, that unethe became there area

For me to stonde, so ful become al the region.

In modern-day English:

"For this turned into on Saint Valentine's Day

When every chicken comes there to select out his suit

Of every type that men may think of

And that so big a noise they started out to make

That earth and air and tree and each lake

Was so whole, that not without issues modified into there place

For me to stand—so full became all of the region."

Readers have uncritically assumed that Chaucer became referring to February 14 as Valentine's Day. Henry Ansgar Kelly has placed that Chaucer could in all likelihood have had in mind the dinner party day of St. Valentine of Genoa, an early bishop of Genoa who died round AD 307; it emerge as probably celebrated on 3 May.A treaty imparting for Richard II and Anne's marriage, the difficulty of the poem, changed into signed on May 2, 1381.

Jack B. Oruch notes that the date on which spring begins offevolved has modified while you keep in mind that Chaucer's time because of the precession of the equinoxes and the arrival of the more accurate Gregorian calendar satisfactory in 1582. On the Julian calendar in use in Chaucer's time, February 14 may additionally want to have fallen on the date now known as February 23, a time whilst a few birds have started out mating and nesting in England.

Chaucer's Parliament of Fowls refers to a supposedly installed way of life, however there may be no file of this kind of way of life earlier than Chaucer. The speculative derivation of gentle customs from the far flung past started out with 18th-century antiquaries, considerably Alban Butler, the writer of Butler's Lives of Saints, and were perpetuated even by means of manner of respectable current-day college students. Most significantly, "the concept that Valentine's Day customs perpetuated the ones of the Roman Lupercalia has been established uncritically and repeated, in severa bureaucracy, as masses as the prevailing".

Three superb authors who made poems about birds mating on St. Valentine's Day across the equal years: Otton de Grandson from Savoy, John Gower from England, and a knight known as Pardo from Valencia. Chaucer maximum probably predated they all; however due to the trouble of relationship medieval works, it isn't possible to fathom which of the four may moreover have brought about the others.

Chapter 14: Symbol Of Love

The earliest description of February 14 as an annual birthday celebration of affection appears inside the Charter of the Court of Love. The charter, allegedly issued thru Charles VI of France at Mantes-l. A.-Jolie in 1400, describes lavish festivities to be attended via manner of severa contributors of the royal courtroom docket, along with a dinner party, amorous music and poetry competitions, jousting and dancing.Amid the ones festivities, the attending ladies need to pay attention and rule on disputes from fans. No precise record of the courtroom docket exists, and none of these named in the charter have been gift at Mantes except Charles's queen, Isabeau of Bavaria, who can also nicely have imagined it all while ready out a deadly disease.

Valentine Poetry

The earliest surviving valentine is a fifteenth-century rondeau written via Charles, Duke of Orléans to his associate, which commences.

"Je suis desja d'amour tanné

Ma tres doulce Valentinée…"

Charles d'Orléans, Rondeau VI, traces 1–2

At the time, the duke become being held within the Tower of London following his seize on the Battle of Agincourt, 1415.

The earliest surviving valentines in English appear like those inside the Paston Letters, written in 1477 thru Margery Brewes to her destiny husband John Paston "my right well-loved Valentine".

Valentine's Day is referred to ruefully with the aid of using Ophelia in William Shakespeare's Hamlet (1600–1601):

"To-morrow is Saint Valentine's day,

All inside the morning betime,

And I a maid at your window,

To be your Valentine.

Then up he rose, and donn'd his clothes,

And dupp'd the chamber-door;

Let in the maid, that out a maid

Never departed greater."

William Shakespeare, Hamlet, Act IV, Scene 5
it

Poet John Donne used the legend of the marriage of the birds because the region to begin for his epithalamion celebrating the marriage of Elizabeth, daughter of James I of England, and Frederick V, Elector Palatine, on Valentine's Day:

"Hayle Bishop Valentine whose day that is

All the Ayre is thy Diocese

And all of the chirping Queristers

And exceptional birds ar thy parishioners

Thou marryest each yeare

The Lyrick Lark, and the graue whispering Doue,

The Sparrow that neglects his existence for loue,

The houshold bird with the redd stomacher

Thou makst the Blackbird speede as soone,

As doth the Goldfinch, or the Halcyon

The Husband Cock lookes out and soone is spedd

And meets his partner, which brings her feather-mattress.

This day more cheerfully than ever shine

This day which might in all likelihood inflame thy selfe vintage Valentine."

John Donne, Epithalamion Vpon Frederick Count Palatine and the Lady Elizabeth marryed on St. Valentines day

The verse "Roses are purple" echoes conventions traceable as a protracted manner over again as Edmund Spenser's epic The Faerie Queene (1590):

"She bath'd with roses purple, and violets blew,

And all of the sweetest flowres [sic], that in the forrest grew.

The contemporary cliché Valentine's Day poem may be determined in Gammer Gurton's Garland (1784), a set of English nursery rhymes posted in London through the use of Joseph Johnson:

"The rose is pink, the violet's blue,

The honey's sweet, and so are you.

Thou artwork my love and I am thine;

I drew thee to my Valentine:

The lot emerge as cast after which I drew,

And Fortune stated it shou'd be you.

Modern Times :An English Victorian generation Valentine card in the Museum of London

In 1797, a British creator issued The Young Man's Valentine Writer, which contained ratings of recommended sentimental verses for the more youthful lover unable to compose his personal. Printers had already commenced producing a limited sort of playing playing cards with verses and sketches, called "mechanical valentines." Paper Valentines have become so famous in England inside the early 19th century that they've been assembled in factories. Fancy Valentines had been made with actual lace and ribbons, with paper lace added within the mid-nineteenth century. In 1835, 60,000 Valentine gambling playing cards were sent through publish inside the United Kingdom, regardless of postage being luxurious.

A reduction in postal costs following Sir Rowland Hill's postal reforms with the 1840 invention of the postage stamp (Penny Black) observed the range of Valentines posted increase, with four hundred,000 despatched simply 3 hundred and sixty 5 days after its invention, and ushered inside the a good buy much less personal however less complex exercising of mailing Valentines.That made it feasible for the number one time to alternate gambling cards anonymously, this is taken due to the truth the reason for the unexpected appearance of racy verse in an era otherwise prudishly Victorian.Production accelerated, "Cupid's Manufactory" as Charles Dickens termed it, with over 3,000 women hired in manufacturing. The Laura Seddon Greeting Card Collection at Manchester Metropolitan University gathers 450 Valentine's Day playing playing playing cards relationship from early nineteenth century Britain, posted through the principal publishers of the day. The series seems in Seddon's e-book Victorian Valentines (1996).

In the usa, the number one carefully produced Valentines of embossed paper lace had been produced and acquired rapidly after 1847 via Esther Howland (1828–1904) of Worcester, Massachusetts. Her father operated a huge ebook and stationery hold, but Howland took her perception from an

English Valentine she had received from a business associate of her father.Impressed with the concept of creating comparable Valentines, Howland started out out her business enterprise via way of importing paper lace and floral decorations from England.

A writer in Graham's American Monthly placed in 1849, "Saint Valentine's Day ... is becoming, nay it has emerge as, a country wide holyday.The English workout of sending Valentine's gambling playing cards modified into installed enough to function as a plot device in Elizabeth Gaskell's Mr. Harrison's Confessions (1851): "I burst in with my reasons: 'The valentine I understand no longer something approximately.' 'It is for your handwriting', stated he coldly. Since 2001, the Greeting Card Association has been giving an annual "Esther Howland Award for a Greeting Card Visionary".

Since the nineteenth century, handwritten notes have given way to heavily produced greeting playing cards.In the United Kingdom, clearly below half of of of the population spend money on their Valentines, and round £1.Nine billion changed into spent in 2015 on cards, flowers, candies and different offers.The mid-19th century Valentine's Day exchange became a harbinger of similarly commercialized vacations within the U.S. To examine.

In 1868, the British chocolate corporation Cadbury created Fancy Boxes – a embellished location of sweets – inside the form of a coronary coronary coronary heart for Valentine's Day.] Boxes of filled chocolates speedy have grow to be related to the holiday. In the second half of the 20 th century, the exercise of replacing playing cards have become extended to all manner of gadgets, which include giving earrings.

The U.S. Greeting Card Association estimates that approximately a hundred ninety million valentines are despatched every year in the US. Half of these valentines are given to circle of relatives people apart from husband or partner, typically to youngsters. When the valentine-trade playing playing playing cards made in college sports activities are protected the determine is going up to one thousand million, and teachers become the people receiving the maximum valentines.The common valentine's spending has extended every one year in the U.S, from $108 a person in 2010 to $131 in 2013.

The rise of Internet recognition at the flip of the millennium is growing new traditions. Millions of people use, each yr, digital manner of creating and sending Valentine's Day greeting messages which includes e-playing cards, love coupons or printable greeting playing playing cards. Valentine's Day is taken into consideration through a few to be a Hallmark holiday because of its commercialization.

Chapter 15: Valentine's Day Reputation World Huge

Valentine's Day customs – sending greeting gambling playing cards (known as "valentines"), presenting confectionery and imparting vegetation – developed in early current England and spread at some point of the English-speakme global inside the nineteenth century. In the later 20th and early twenty first centuries, the ones customs spread to exclusive international locations, much like the ones of Halloween, or than elements of Christmas, (consisting of Santa Claus).

Valentine's Day is well known in plenty of East Asian global locations with Singaporeans, Chinese and South Koreans spending the maximum cash on Valentine's provides.

Americas

Latin America

In maximum Latin American worldwide locations, as an instance, Costa Rica, Mexico, and the U.S. Territory of Puerto Rico, Saint Valentine's Day is known as Día de los Enamorados ('Day of Lovers')[93] or as Día del Amor y l. A. Amistad ('Day of Love and Friendship'). It is likewise not unusual to look human beings carry out "acts of appreciation" for his or her pals.

In Guatemala it's miles referred to as Día del Cariño ('Affection Day'). Some worldwide places, specially the Dominican Republic and El Salvador,have a way of life known as Amigo secreto ("Secret friend"), it really is a sport similar to the Christmas life-style of Secret Santa.

Brazil

Main article: Dia dos Namorados

In Brazil, the Dia dos Namorados (lit. "Lovers' Day", or "Boyfriends'/Girlfriends' Day") is widely recognized on June 12, likely because of the truth that is the day earlier than Saint Anthony's day, appeared there because of the reality the 'marriage saint',[citation needed] while historically many unmarried girls perform well-known rituals, known as simpatias, as a manner to discover a suitable husband or boyfriend. Couples exchange objects, goodies, gambling cards, and flower bouquets. The February 14 Valentine's Day isn't celebrated in any respect as it commonly falls too little earlier than or too little after the Brazilian Carnival – that may fall everywhere from early February to early March and lasts almost each week. Because of the absence of Valentine's Day and because of the celebrations of the Carnivals, Brazil changed into recommended thru U.S. News & World Report as a traveller vacation spot inside the direction of February for Western singles who want to interrupt out from the vacation.

Colombia

Colombia celebrates Día del amor y los angeles amistad at the 0.33 Saturday in September rather.Amigo Secreto is likewise famous there.

United States

On the us mainland, approximately a hundred ninety million Valentine's Day playing playing cards are sent every year, no longer which include the hundreds of hundreds of thousands of playing playing playing cards school youngsters trade.

Valentine's Day is a primary supply of monetary pastime, with present day costs in 2017 topping $18.2 billion in 2017, or over $136 consistent with individual. This is an growth from $108 consistent with individual in 2010. In 2019, a survey with the aid of the National Retail Federation decided that over the preceding decade, the percentage of these who've an splendid time Valentine's Day had declined regularly. From their survey outcomes, they determined 3 primary reasons: over-commercialization of the holiday, no longer having a large unique, and no longer being interested by celebrating it.

Asia

Afghanistan

In pre-Taliban years Koch-e-Gul-Faroushi (Flower Street) within the down city Kabul changed into embellished with revolutionary flower arrangements to attract Valentine's Day celebrating kids.In the Afghan culture, love is regularly expressed through poetry. Some new technology budding poets like Ramin Mazhar, Mahtab Sahel are expressing themselves through poetry the usage of Valentine's Day expressing troubles on any opportunity of erosion of freedoms. In their political remark they defy fear through way of pronouncing I kiss you amid the Taliban.

Bangladesh

Main article: Valentine's Day in Bangladesh

Valentine's Day modified into first celebrated in Bangladesh via Shafik Rehman, a journalist and editor of Jaijaidin in 1993. He have emerge as acquainted with Western tradition through using manner of analyzing in London.He highlighted Valentine's Day to the

Bangladeshi humans thru Jaijaidin newspaper. Rehman is known as the "father of Valentine's Day in Bangladesh".On within the suggest time, human beings in numerous bonds which incorporates fans, pals, husbands and better halves, moms and kids, college students and instructors unique their love for each different with flowers, candies, playing playing cards and different offers. On in recent times, numerous parks and task centers of america of a are entire of human beings of love.No public holiday is declared in this day in Bangladesh.

Some in Bangladesh revel in that celebrating these days isn't acceptable from a cultural and Islamic factor of view. Before the celebration of Valentine's Day, February 14 was celebrated because the anti-authoritarian day in Bangladesh. However, that day is overlooked via human beings to have a laugh Valentine's Day.

China

In Chinese, Valentine's Day is called lovers' festival (simplified Chinese: 情人节; traditional Chinese: 情人節; Mandarin: Qīng Rén Jié; Hokkien: Chêng Lîn Chiat; Cantonese: Chìhng Yàhn Jit; Shanghainese Xin Yin Jiq). The "Chinese Valentine's Day" is the Qixi Festival (this means that "The Night of Sevens" (Chinese: 七夕; pinyin: Qi Xi)), celebrated at the seventh day of the 7th month of the lunar calendar. According to the legend, the Cowherd superstar and the Weaver Maid movie star are commonly separated by manner of manner of the Milky Way (silvery river) however are allowed to meet with the aid of crossing it on the 7th day of the seventh month of the Chinese calendar.

In contemporary-day years, celebrating White Day has moreover emerge as elegant amongst a few young humans.

India

Main article: Valentine's Day in India

In historic India, there has been a way of life of adoring Kamadeva, the lord of affection exemplified with the beneficial resource of the erotic carvings inside the Khajuraho Group of Monuments and thru the writing of the Kamasutra. This lifestyle modified into out of region during the Middle Ages, even as Kamadeva changed into not celebrated, and public shows of sexual affection have become frowned upon.This repression of public affections began out to loosen in the Nineteen Nineties.

Valentine's Day celebrations did not lure on in India until round 1992. It turned into spread because of the programs in commercial TV channels, together with MTV, devoted radio programs, and love letter competitions, similarly to a fee-effective liberalization that allowed the explosion of the valentine card company.The birthday celebration has precipitated a pointy trade on how people have been displaying their affection in public because the Middle Ages.

On a 2018 on line survey, it have become located that 68% of the respondents do not desire to have a laugh Valentine's Day. It may be additionally located that one-of-a-kind religious businesses, collectively with Hindu,Muslim and Christian humans of India do not guide Valentine's Day.

In present day times, Hindu and Islamic traditionalists have considered the vacation to be cultural contamination from the West, a end result of globalization in India.Shiv Sena and the Sangh Parivar have asked their followers to shun the vacation and the "public admission of affection" due to them being "alien to Indian way of life".Although the ones protests are prepared with the aid of political elites, the protesters themselves are center-elegance Hindu men who worry that the globalization will ruin the traditions of their society: prepared marriages, Hindu joint households, entire-time mothers, and masses of others. Despite those barriers, Valentine's Day is becoming an increasing number of well-known in India.

Valentine's Day has been strongly criticized from a postcolonial angle via intellectuals from the Indian left. The excursion is regarded as a the the front for "Western imperialism", "neocolonialism", and "the exploitation of running instructions via commercialism via multinational agencies". It is said that due to Valentine's Day, the working instructions and rural horrific come to be extra disconnected socially, politically, and geographically from the hegemonic capitalist energy form. They furthermore criticize mainstream media attacks on Indians against Valentine's Day as a shape of demonization this is designed and derived to in addition the Valentine's Day time desk. Right wing Hindu nationalists also are opposed. In February 2012, Subash Chouhan of the Bajrang Dal warned couples that "They can't kiss or hug in public locations. Our activists will beat them up". He said "We are not in opposition to love, however we criticize vulgar exhibition of affection at public locations".

The history of Valentine's Day in Iran dates once more to the Qajar technology of the latter half of of the 19th century—Naser al-Din Shah Qajar did no longer take his spouse with him at some stage in his revel in to Europe and he despatched her a greeting card from distance on Valentine's Day. This greeting card is available in Iranian museums.

Since the mid-2000s, Valentine's Day has grow to be increasingly well-known in Iran, in particular amongst young people. However, it has furthermore been the problem of heavy grievance from Iranian conservatives, who see it as a part of the spread of "decadent" Western tradition.Since 2011, authorities have attempted to discourage celebrations and impose regulations on the sale and production of Valentine's Day-associated items, regardless of the truth that the holiday remains well-known as of 2018.] Additionally, there have been efforts to restore the ancient Persian opposition of Sepandārmazgān, which takes place throughout the same time, to replace Valentine's Day, even though, as of

2016, this has additionally been in large part unsuccessful.

Israel

In Israel, the Jewish way of life of Tu B'Av has been revived and converted into the Jewish equal of Valentine's Day. It is widely recognized at the 15th day of the month of Av (commonly in overdue August). In historical instances ladies might located on white garb and dance inside the vineyards, in which the men might be looking for them (Mishna Taanith give up of Chapter four). Today, Tu B'Av is nicely referred to as a 2d vacation of love via manner of secular human beings (in conjunction with Valentine's Day), and it shares a number of the customs related to Saint Valentine's Day in western societies. In present day Israeli culture Tu B'Av is a famous day to proclaim love, advise marriage, and deliver objects like playing cards or plant life.

Japan

In Japan, Morozoff Ltd. Introduced the vacation for the number one time in 1936, on the identical time as it ran an industrial geared in the direction of foreigners. Later, in 1953, it commenced out promoting the giving of coronary coronary heart-original sweets; other Japanese confectionery businesses decided wholesome thereafter. In 1958, the Isetan department hold ran a "Valentine sale". Further campaigns in some unspecified time in the future of the Sixties popularized the custom.

The custom that most effective girls supply goodies to men can also have originated from the interpretation errors of a chocolate-corporation government sooner or later of the initial campaigns.] In precise, administrative center ladies deliver chocolate to their co-people. Unlike western international locations, gadgets which includes greeting cards,[138] candies, plants, or dinner dates are uncommon, and maximum of the presents-related hobby is prepared giving the right quantity of chocolate to anyone.Japanese chocolate agencies make half of their annual income during this time of the 12 months.

Many ladies experience obliged to provide chocolates to all male co-people, besides while the day falls on a Sunday, a holiday. This is known as giri-choko (義理チョコ), from 'giri' ("obligation") and 'choko', ("chocolate"), with unpopular co-humans receiving exceptional "extraordinarily-obligatory" (超義理チョコ 'chō-giri choko') reasonably-priced chocolate. This contrasts with honmei-choko (本命チョコ, lit. "actual feeling chocolate"), chocolate given to a loved one. Friends, particularly girls, can also additionally alternate chocolate known as tomo-choko (友チョコ, from 'tomo' because of this that "buddy").

In the Nineteen Eighties, the Japanese National Confectionery Industry Association released a successful advertising campaign to make March 14 a "respond day", wherein men are anticipated to go lower back the favour to people who gave them sweets on Valentine's Day, calling it White Day for the coloration of the chocolates being provided. A previous failed attempt to popularize this birthday celebration were finished through the use of a marshmallow producer who desired men to transport again marshmallows to girls.

In Japan, the romantic "date night time" associated with Valentine's Day is widely identified on Christmas Eve.

United Kingdom

Valentine's Day love notes on display in 2010 for creating a charitable donation to the British Heart Foundation

In the United Kingdom, simply under half of of the populace spends coins on their Valentines and round £1.Three billion is spent every year on gambling cards, vegetation, candies, and special affords, with an anticipated 25 million gambling cards being despatched.

In Wales, a few human beings have a very good time Dydd Santes Dwynwen (St. Dwynwen's Day) on January 25 in preference to (or in addition to) Valentine's Day. The day commemorates St Dwynwen, the Welsh customer saint of love.The Welsh name for Saint Valentine is Sant Ffolant.

In a 2016 poll carried out by means of the usage of Channel 4 for Valentine's Day, Jane Austen's line, "My coronary heart is, and usually may be, yours", from her novel Sense and Sensibility as stated via Edward Ferrars (Hugh Grant) to Elinor Dashwood (Emma Thompson) in the acclaimed 1995 movie version, changed into voted

the maximum romantic line from literature, movie, and TV thru masses

Philippines

In the Philippines, Valentine's Day is known as Araw ng mga Puso in masses the equal manner as inside the West. It is generally marked through way of a steep growth in the charge of flora, in particular purple roses.It is the most well-known day for weddings. With a few localities presenting mass ceremonies for no price.

Saudi Arabia

In Saudi Arabia, in 2002 and 2008, religious police banned the sale of all Valentine's Day gadgets, telling keep personnel to cast off any purple items, due to the reality the day is considered a Christian holiday This ban has created a black marketplace for roses and wrapping paper. In 2012, the religious police arrested extra than 140 Muslims for celebrating the holiday, and confiscated all purple roses from flower stores.Muslims are not prison to have a laugh the vacation, and non-Muslims can have fun simplest within the decrease returned of closed doors.

"Saudi cleric Sheikh Muhammad Al-'Arifi said on Valentine's Day Eve that celebrating this vacation constitutes bid'a – a forbidden innovation and deviation from religious law and custom – and mimicry of the West."

However, in 2017 and 2018, after a fatwa changed into in huge component circulated, the religious police did not prevent Muslims from celebrating the day. In 2018, Sheikh Ahmed Qasim Al-Ghamdi, a Saudi cleric and previous president of the Committee for the Promotion of Virtue and Prevention of Vice, stated that Valentine's Day isn't haram and is well matched with Islamic values.

Singapore

According to findings, Singaporeans are among the most important spenders on Valentine's Day, with 60% of Singaporeans indicating that they may spend among $100 and $500 in some unspecified time in the future of the season leading as a whole lot as the vacation.

Europe

Estonia and Finland

In Finland, Valentine's Day is referred to as ystävänpäivä, because of this that that "Friend's Day". As the decision indicates, in the meanwhile is more approximately remembering buddies, no longer tremendous others. In Estonia, Valentine's Day have end up first of all called valentinipäev and later additionally sõbrapäev ('Friend's Day') as a calque of the Finnish term.

France

In France, a traditionally Catholic united states of the united states, Valentine's Day is idea genuinely as "Saint Valentin", and is widely known in plenty the equal manner as distinctive western worldwide locations. The relics of Saint Valentin de Terni, the consumer of the St Valentine's Day, are within the Catholic church of Saint-Jean-Baptiste and Saint-Jean-l'Evangéliste located inside the southern France town of Roquemaure, Gard. The celebrations of "Fête des Amoureux" takes vicinity every two years at the Sunday closest to February 14. The village receives wearing its 19th-century costume and placed at the utility with over 800 human beings.

Greece

St. Valentine's Day, or Ημέρα του Αγίου Βαλεντίνου in Greek manner of existence have come to be now not associated with romantic love. In the Eastern Orthodox church there can be another Saint who protects people who are in love, Hyacinth of Caesarea (dinner party day July three), however this become not broadly diagnosed until the late Nineties . In current Greece, Valentine's Day is typically celebrated as inside the not unusual Western subculture.

IRELAND

On Saint Valentine's Day in Ireland, many folks that are searching out authentic love make a Christian pilgrimage to the Shrine of St. Valentine in Whitefriar Street Carmelite Church in Dublin, that is said to residence relics of Saint Valentine of Rome; they pray at the shrine in preference of locating romance.There lies a ebook wherein foreigners and locals have written their prayer requests for love.

Poland

Saint Valentine's Day have come to be introduced to Poland together with the cult of Saint Valentine thru Bavaria and Tyrol.However, it rose in popularity inside the Nineteen Nineties. The most effective (and the most critical) public birthday celebration in Poland is held yearly from 2002 in Chełmn ounder the call „Walentynki Chełmińskie" (Chełmno Valentine's). Because Chełmno's parish church of the Assumption of the Blessed Virgin Mary has been preserving the relic of St. Valentine for the motive that Middle Ages, neighborhood cult of the saint has been mixed with the Anglo-Saxon way of life.

Portugal

In Portugal, the vacation is called "Dia dos Namorados" (Lover's Day / Day of the Enamoured). As some place else, couples change offers, but in a few areas, girls supply a lenço de namorados ("lovers' handkerchief"), this is generally embroidered with love motifs.

Romania

In modern-day years, Romania has additionally began out celebrating Valentine's Day. This has drawn backlash from severa businesses, establishments,and nationalist agencies like Noua Dreaptă, who condemn Valentine's Day for being superficial, commercialist, and imported Western kitsch. In order to counter the perceived denaturation of country wide manner of life, Dragobete, a spring competition celebrated in additives of Southern Romania, has been rekindled after having been omitted at some degree within the Communist years because of the truth the traditional Romanian excursion for fanatics. The vacation is called after a person from Romanian folklore who turn out to be alleged to be the son of Baba Dochia. Its date used to vary counting on the geographical location, however these days it's far usually positioned on February 24.

Scandinavia

In Denmark and Norway, February 14 is known as Valentinsdag, and is well known in a bargain the equal way as in the United Kingdom.In Sweden it is referred to as Alla hjärtans dag ("All Hearts' Day") but isn't in big component elebrated. A 2016 survey decided that a bargain much less than 50% of males and females were planning to buy provides for their partners. The vacation has only been discovered for the reason that 1960s.

Spain

The excursion become first brought in Spain through a 1948 industrial marketing campaign with the resource of the branch preserve chain Galerías Preciados,and had become massive with the resource of the Seventies.

Known as "San Valentín", the vacation is widely known the same way as within the relaxation of the West.

Restrictions in some countries.

The birthday celebration of Valentine's Day has been banned in Indonesia, Pakistan, and

Saudi Arabia because of ideals the holiday conflicts with Islamic way of life.

Since 2009, certain practices relating Valentine's Day (along with giving plants, playing gambling playing cards, or one-of-a-type items suggestive of Valentine's Day) are banned in Iran. Iran's Law Enforcement Force prosecutes corporations of merchandise with symbols related to Valentine's Day.In 2021, the Prosecutor's Office of Qom, Iran, stated that it will prosecute folks who disseminate and offer anti-cultural symbols like the ones of Valentine's Day

Although Valentine's Day is not sizeable or authorized through any employer in Iran and has no professional repute, it's especially commonplace amongst a massive a part of the population. One of the motives for Valentine's Day popularity for the cause that 2000s by way of manner of the overall population is the trade in family members the various genders, and because of the reality sexual courting aren't strictly restricted to be within marriage.

Chapter 16: The History Of Valentine's Day

In honour of St. Valentine, cherished ones alternate candy, flowers, and presents anywhere within the worldwide and in the United States. But who's this enigmatic saint, and wherein did those customs originate? Learn about Valentine's Day's which means and records, from the historical Roman ritual of Luplercalia, which marked the begin of spring, to Victorian England's card-giving traditions.

According to a few assets, Saint Valentine is truely incredible historic figures who're stated to have cured a toddler at the same time as they have been imprisoned and decapitated.

Where Did The Holiday Of Love Originate?

The tour's origins and client saint's story are shrouded in mystery. We do realize that Valentine's Day, as we recognize it in recent times, is rooted in Christian and historic Roman customs, and that February has lengthy been celebrated as a month of affection. But who've end up Saint Valentine, and the manner did he come to be associated with this eon-antique rite?

Valentine or Valentinus is the name of at least three outstanding saints, all of whom have been martyred, consistent with the Catholic Church. According to as a minimum one legend, Valentine changed into a clergyman who lived in Rome inside the zero.33 century. Young men were forbidden from marrying whilst Emperor Claudius II determined that single guys have been higher soldiers than humans with families and better halves. Confronted with the injustice of the decree, Valentine defied Claudius and persisted to secretly wed more youthful fans. Claudius ordered Valentine's execution at the same time as his actions had been discovered. Still others contend that the real purchaser saint of the holiday became a bishop named Saint Valentine of Terni. Outside of Rome, Claudius II finished him as nicely.

Valentine also can moreover had been killed, regular with superb debts, for trying to help Christians in escaping the cruel Roman prisons, in which they had been regularly crushed and tortured. One legend states that an imprisoned Valentine despatched the primary "valentine" greeting himself after falling in love with a more youthful lady who visited him during his confinement, probably his jailor's daughter. It is stated that he despatched her a letter in advance than his lack of existence which have end up signed "From your Valentine," a phrase this is even though used these days. Despite the paradox of the legends surrounding Valentine, all of them emphasise his attraction as a sympathetic, heroic, and, most importantly, romantic figure. Valentine ought to rise to prominence as one of the maximum loved saints in England and France with the resource of the use of the Middle Ages, probable because of this popularity.

The History Of Valentine's Day

A Pagan Festival in February While a few human beings do not forget that Valentine's Day is located in the middle of February to mark the anniversary of Valentine's loss of life or burial, which maximum probable befell spherical 270 A.D., others contend that the Christian church can also have selected to study Valentine's Day in the middle of February that allows you to "Christianize" the pagan competition of Lupercalia. Lupercalia became a fertility opposition hung on the ides of February, or February 15, and it have grow to be committed to Faunus, the Roman god of agriculture, similarly to to Romulus and Remus, the Roman founders.

The Luperci, a tough and fast of Roman clergymen, might probably accumulate in a sacred cave in which it modified into believed that a she-wolf or sorted Romulus and Remus once they had been infants to kick off the opposition. A goat changed into sacrificed for fertility, and a canine changed into sacrificed for purification, through the monks. After that, they could lessen the goat's cover into strips, dip them within the blood of the sacrifice, and then take to the streets to softly slap women further to farmers within the fields with the goat hide. Roman women did now not worry the touch of the hides as it become believed to growth their fertility in the coming three hundred and sixty five days. Legend says that every one the younger women in the town could positioned their names in a big urn later that day. The metropolis's bachelors ought to every choose a call and be paired with the girl in their desire for the yr. Marriage grow to be often the result of those suits.

Lupercalia turn out to be legalised on the surrender of the fifth century at the same time as Pope Gelasius made February 14 St. Valentine's Day as it modified into deemed "un-Christian." Although it survived the early upward thrust of Christianity, Lupercalia have become outlawed. However, it wasn't till a good deal later that the day become definitively associated with love. During the Middle Ages, it became common information in France and England that February 14 marked the begin of the breeding season for birds. This added to the belief that Valentine's Day need to be celebrated inside the center of February. "For this became sent on Saint Valentine's day / When every foul cometh thee to pick his mate," Geoffrey Chaucer, an English poet, wrote in his 1375 poem "Parliament of Foules," come to be the primary to explain Valentine's Day as an afternoon of birthday party for enthusiasts.

Although written Valentines did not start to appear until after the twelve months 1400, Valentine greetings were drastically used in the Middle Ages. A poem that Charles, Duke of Orleans, wrote to his wife in 1415 at the identical time as he end up held captive in the Tower of London following his seize on the Battle of Agincourt is the oldest Valentine's Day although in life. The greeting is now inside the British Library's manuscript series in London, England.) It is concept that King Henry V employed a author named John Lydgate to put in writing a valentine's have a look at for Catherine of Valois numerous years later.

Who Is Cupid?

On Valentine's Day gambling cards, Cupid is regularly depicted as a naked cherub hurling love arrows at fanatics who aren't paying interest. However, the Greek god of affection, Eros, gave shipping to the Roman God Cupid. His begin tale varies; Some claim that Nyx and Erebus are his parents; others, which include Ares and Aphrodite; He may be the son of Iris and Zephyrus or perhaps Aphrodite and Zeus, who might have been his father and grandfather, consistent with distinctive theories.